ANGER MANAGEMENT FOR MEN

A Self-Help Anger Management Guide for When a Man Has Anger Issues

Riley Hunt

© Copyright 2023 - All rights reserved.

The content contained within this book may not be reproduced, duplicated or transmitted without direct written permission from the author or the publisher.

Under no circumstances will any blame or legal responsibility be held against the publisher, or author, for any damages, reparation, or monetary loss due to the information contained within this book, either directly or indirectly.

Legal Notice:

This book is copyright protected. It is only for personal use. You cannot amend, distribute, sell, use, quote or paraphrase any part, or the content within this book, without the consent of the author or publisher.

Disclaimer Notice:

Please note the information contained within this document is for educational and entertainment purposes only. All effort has been executed to present accurate, up to date, reliable, complete information. No warranties of any kind are declared or implied. Readers acknowledge that the author is not engaged in the rendering of legal, financial, medical or professional advice. The content within this book has been derived from various sources. Please consult a licensed professional before attempting any techniques outlined in this book.

By reading this document, the reader agrees that under no circumstances is the author responsible for any losses, direct or indirect, that are incurred as a result of the use of the information contained within this document, including, but not limited to, errors, omissions, or inaccuracies.

TABLE OF CONTENTS

Do you love FREE things?

Get your free book today!

Conflict Resolution: Stories from Men

https://bit.ly/3SMFUdc

OR

SCAN ME

INTRODUCTION

Anger is like a fire that never burns out. Sometimes it looks like just a few glowing embers; other times, it can engulf a house.

What is anger? The simple answer is that it's when you're feeling mad. The extended answer is likely what started your search for help with anger management. While everyone experiences anger from time to time, what you're dealing with might feel a little different. Anger can have a negative impact on your emotional, physical, and social health.

Anger is one of the most stigmatized emotions and can look different in men. As a man, you have a job and family to balance and a reputation to uphold. You might be at a point in your life where you can easily see how your anger has had a negative impact on your life, yet for some reason, it's still a struggle to understand how to control those emotional reactions.

The relationship between men and emotions is a complicated one. Everyone feels emotions, yet there are certain expectations placed on men in our society, which can lead to the fear of showing these emotions. Fear, depression, and other basic human reactions don't go away just because you aren't expressing them. Instead, these thoughts and feelings are internalized. You are only one person, however, and eventually, that pressure will release in some way.Anger demands a response, and if you are not focused on emotional management, that response is often unfavorable. While it might feel like there is a small release of anger in that moment, the cleanup is often messier than the initial incident that started the explosion. What does this look like in your life? A broken relationship? Physical or mental harm? A ruined career or reputation?

Anger can be one of the most contradictory feelings we have. When people are displaying intense anger like rage, they often try to appear powerful, maybe even trying to exert control over those around them. Think about someone who pulls a gun in a road rage incident or a boyfriend who throws a glass in the direction of his girlfriend. This display of control isn't there because the angry person actually has the power. In reality, this type of explosive anger is often masking a deeper emotion. For example, anger often masks fear.

To understand this, picture your geographical location. How close are you to predatory animals? If you're in the Everglades of Florida, this might look like an alligator. If you are in the mountains of New Jersey, this might be a bear. Now imagine that you go for a walk in nature, only to stumble into the territory of one of these predatory animals. There's a good chance that they would show signs of aggression, especially if they are protecting their young. Bears growl, alligators show their teeth, and gorillas pound their chest. They won't outright attack unless they are feeling especially threatened. This is because, deep down, they still have fear. They want to protect themselves and their cubs, and they are displaying these reactions to show those around them that they are not afraid.

This reaction is a survival tactic! It provides a necessary urgency to the rest of the body based on a perceived threat. While humans have much more emotional control than these species, at the end of the day, we are still animals ourselves. Our emotions can be contradictory because our response might be the opposite of the truth. How many times have you said, "I'm fine," or "It's fine," when deep down, you were afraid of the future? Even admitting that there is any fear hiding underneath the surface can be difficult for men to admit.

You might be thinking, "What about when I'm just annoyed at those around me?" or "What about when someone is simply being disrespectful?"

Not all anger is rooted in fear. It's a complex emotion, and these are just some of the most common examples. There are plenty of times when you might be feeling frustrated and not fearful, like if your child is endlessly playing with a repetitive, noisy toy, or if your coworker won't stop talking loudly on the phone in the breakroom. Throughout this book, I will discuss the complexities of anger and why these feelings arise. As someone who has experienced anger issues my entire life, I know how much anger can negatively impact all parts of our lives. Whether it's our family, job, or social life, letting our emotions get the best of us can have detrimental effects. Through research, therapy, and practice, I have been able to resolve some of the underlying issues of anger and have learned to control my anger both at work and home. I'm here to help you come up with a plan so that you can take back power over anger.

Those who are angry are responding to an emotion, but unfortunately, that reaction can often hurt others. This leads to feelings of regret and shame, which are feelings that are also hard for men to express within our society. Fortunately for our generation and our future sons, the social norm of anger has changed over time, so more men are seeking help for their anger management.

Angering situations will always arise, so it can make us feel as though trying to manage those feelings is hopeless. You can't make traffic go away. You won't be able to control thoughtless drivers. There will always be short-staffed and busy restaurants that get your order wrong from time to time. Your relationships won't be 100% free from conflict, and work will always have random stressors.

You can't control your future. However, you do have unequivocal power over your emotions. You can't stop the trigger, but you can choose the response.

The first step in controlling anger is understanding what this emotion really means. Anger triggers lurk around every corner, and it can be hard to know when it's going to pop out of nowhere. Having strategies prepared is the best way to create your defense against anger so that rather than having it control you, you have total power over your responses and reactions.

CHAPTER 1:

What is Anger?

If you strip down this complex emotion to its simplest form, it is a reaction. What is a reaction? A reaction is what occurs after an initial event.

Imagine doing something simple, like dropping a small amount of water into a pan. What happens? The water sizzles and steams. Your ears and eyes pick up on what is happening. These are reactions.

If you drop a heavy object into a bucket of paint, the reaction is a paint explosion in the surrounding area. If you spill water on a newspaper, the reaction is that the ink smears, and the paper becomes soggy. Anger is a reaction that occurs in a situation surrounding us.

You might think that this means anger is not your fault. That's true on some level. Anger is normal, and you can't always help what might trigger you. What matters is your response. That is what anger management is all about; you are the one in charge of how you choose to respond to your emotion.

On the simplest level, anger is the way we react to a perception of a situation, whether it's our physical surroundings or something that emotionally triggers us. Anger feels different for everyone, but it is often viewed as an anxiety-inducing and stressful emotion. Life is stressful, and anyone around you can tell you that anger-inducing issues arise daily. However, letting this simple feeling lead you can be dangerous to all areas of your life.

The first part of anger management is getting a comprehensive understanding of what anger is at the core. To help get your mindset started around healing from anger, first think of yourself as a little boy and how those feelings started to develop. Who taught you how to express your anger? You might be someone who saw poor anger management in a male figure in your life, like a verbally abusive father. You might not have been allowed to express emotion at all, therefore making you more prone to avoidance and explosion. You might not have had any male role model in your life, so you relied on preconceived notions of what anger looks like based on what you saw in society and media.

Any one of these situations can have a deep impact on your life for years to come. Who were your role models for anger, and how did you learn what this emotion manifested itself into? Reflecting on this is an important part of breaking down this emotion so that you can get a better sense of where your relationship with anger issues began.

Anger Is Normal

According to Merriam-Webster (2023), the definition of anger is "a strong feeling of displeasure and usually of antagonism."

Anger is one of the most normal emotions that you will feel. It's important to understand that you are not a bad person if you think of yourself as an angry person. You are not wrong for holding on to anger. You are not broken. It is not a faulty issue in your emotional system.

Every single person that you know has anger. Everyone has lived through moments of anger, and everyone has a moment involving anger that they regret. The severity differs from person to person, but you have to understand that it's an emotion that everybody experiences. It doesn't always seem like this because of the preconceived notions and behavior often associated with anger. The quiet person who never speaks up, that shy person you work with, and your relative who always keeps to themselves have experienced anger. The exciting and happy person who is always laughing has experienced anger. Everybody shows it in different ways, and everybody holds on to it in unique patterns.

Fight-Or-Flight Response

Anger is related to our fear response. Humans are animals and, like many species, we have a fight or flight response. This response is why birds flutter away when you walk past a group of them on the sidewalk. It's why a rat will scurry if you spot it near the dumpster. It's the reason that a spider might bite you when it's crawling up your leg. All species have different biological responses as to how they react to a threat.

As you might know from your own experiences, this reaction doesn't always have the best results. For example, a deer might freeze and stare directly into headlights as a huge truck is speeding toward it in the middle of the road. What ends up happening is that the deer and the person in the car end up getting hurt. However, this was a reaction that the deer had based on natural senses and past experiences. When a deer stops and freezes, its body is telling it not to move since it cannot see the things around it. Confusion around the source of the light arises, and it tries to make sense of its surroundings.

When we have our own emotional reactions, our bodies try to help us to do the best thing in the moment. Unfortunately, some situations bring about immediate regret. The saying hindsight is 20/20 refers to how sometimes you don't know what the best thing to do would have been until there is time and distance from the issue. Anger acts as an immediate response because it's what our mind thinks is best right at that moment.

What happens, however, is that the pattern in which we respond to fear becomes repeated and reinforced. Your mind cares about survival and not necessarily ensuring that you thrive. Your mind can sometimes become focused on finding the easiest solution for you to get what you want in a situation. For example, yelling and screaming might get you the things that you want in life because people become afraid of you and are willing to give in. However, that doesn't help you or the people around you thrive in a healthy environment.

Everybody has a fight-or-flight response to an outside stressor. If somebody is calling you names, bullying you, or intentionally harassing you, you might fight them back, or you might run away and try to hide from them. If work is pounding down on you and everything feels overwhelming and threatening, you might flee from your problems and go straight to the bar to bury your sorrows with alcohol. You might also fight them head-on and get mean or angry with your coworkers or your boss.

The fight-or-flight response isn't a bad thing. It's what keeps us safe and makes sure that we're putting our attention where it's needed. However, even misguided responses can get us what we want, so your brain keeps doing it. For example, if you repeatedly get angry at your job, you might make a habit of getting a drink after your shift. It helps alleviate the feeling, but then work comes again, and so does the pain. Your brain remembers that the last time you felt this pain, you had a few drinks, and the pain went away. Your brain will then seek out that pattern because even though alcohol abuse can lead to long-term health issues, it provides immediate relief.

Your mind knows that the bad habits or alleviation techniques you participate in are better than doing nothing at all, even though your brain also recognizes that it's not the best thing to do. When we repeat these patterns over and over again, it becomes even harder for us to break them. Our reactions become normalized, and less effort is put into change because, once again, our brain has taken note that this method keeps working. What anger does to our minds and body can start to have damaging effects.

Being reactionary can take away from your ability to make sound judgments and to know what the best thing to do is in a situation. Anger clouds your judgment, and it affects the way that you think. Knowing how you handle your fight or flight response will give you more power over the way that you cope with this biological reaction.

Chemical Reaction

This fight-or-flight response also creates a chemical reaction in your body. Your body is kicking off a hormonal process to help you get the things that you need in order to achieve survival. What this looks like is a release of hormones such as adrenaline and testosterone. This readies your body so that you can either run away as fast as you can or fight as hard as you can. Your muscles will tense up, and your heart will start to beat faster. You might even start to sweat to help keep your body temperature regulated. Your muscles tense up so that you can react faster, and your focus and mind become alert to the problem so that you have a clearer picture of the situation.

This all sounds like a long and complex process, but it happens instantly and often without our control. Think about how you quickly catch your balance when slipping on an icy sidewalk, or the way you might quickly duck if you sense something flying towards your head.

Our body never stops pumping blood and regulating hormones, even when we're in deep sleep. How you respond and react to your surroundings changes how your body's chemistry functions. This is an important reminder as we dive deeper into how much anger has affected us up until this point. You choose what to feed your body, when to go to the bathroom, and how much you exercise. Beyond this, how you react to your emotions also affects your health.

While anger is an emotion, your relationship with it can shape who you are.

Understanding Men With Anger Issues

Research shows that women and men feel angry just as frequently as one another (Delvin, 2019). It's not the emotion itself that differs among the sexes, but instead, the reaction that is attached. Anger can show as a response to the inability to "contextualize emotions and understand why you are feeling a certain way" (Delvin, 2019).

Has anyone ever told you to "man up?" Has anybody ever said, "Women are emotional" around you? How many times have you heard that a woman couldn't be president because "She's too emotional," or that a woman must be on her period because she's acting sassy? Women are labeled as the emotional ones even though we, as men, are just as emotional.

Have you seen more men or more women cry in your lifetime? How did your peers, family members, or teachers respond to you or other boys crying? Were the women in your life seen as more emotional? Were the men in your life seen as more aggressive?

Regardless of whether or not there are biological differences between men and women in regard to emotions, it's easy to see that in our society, male emotional expressions aren't as frequently accepted.

Because of this, many men will withdraw from their emotions. This might result in withdrawal from peers, working and leaving home more, and participating in more reckless behavior (Men and Emotions, n.d.).

This development of how anger exists in us goes as far back as childhood age. Your parents played a huge role in how you dealt with emotions as a child, and that can still affect your relationship with emotional expression as an adult. Aside from that, it's also about how your peers express them. Were you in a male-dominated sport surrounded by others that held heightened masculine viewpoints? Were you in a diverse group where you had an equal amount of male and female perspectives? This might change how you share feelings now within your friend group. Your teachers might have also treated you differently based on your sex. Sometimes this is conscious, but sometimes it's just because of how society has passed down beliefs over time. All of this is important to consider as we begin to challenge the idea of how men are able to express emotions in a healthy way.

How We Were Raised

The way that men are raised over time is done both consciously and subconsciously by our caregivers. Choosing to buy little boys trucks and action figures and little girls baby dolls is a conscious choice. Deeper than that are many things that are subconscious. There are certain expectations and beliefs which are ingrained in what we believe as a society. These are passed down over time, and we often participate in rituals related to them without thought.

This isn't to demonize tradition but instead to look at the way that we have been raised differently over time.

The subconscious methods of parenting little boys can have long-term effects on how they deal with emotions as men. For example, the way a teacher responds to a little boy or little girl crying might be different. What things grandparents or even strangers in the grocery store say to kids can also change how they are perceived and how they view themselves.

Not everything that we do is a conscious choice, and a lot of how we interact and behave with others is taught to us through society and continues to be upheld through generations. Again, traditional gender roles don't have to be either good or bad; the main point is that issues with anger can stem back deep into our childhood. In addition, much of this upbringing was out of our control, which serves as a reminder that we can't keep ourselves stuck in guilt over how we were raised. We were children, and what we were taught isn't our fault.

What is valuable with this information now is that we can use it to trace the stems of our issues back to the very root. Once we are able to find the source, it will be easier to know how to overcome some of the deep obstacles that feel ingrained into our psyche.

The Pressure on Men

Anger has a greater impact on men because of the pressures that are placed on them in society. Men are supposed to be the head of the household and uphold certain standards as friends, brothers, fathers, sons, and husbands.

This pressure is incredibly intense, especially with the lack of resources that our society presents to help men feel safe with themselves and their feelings. In addition, there is a guilt that is placed on men when they feel emotional, so even if there are resources available, they might be afraid to speak up and share this with others.

Men are often more likely to struggle with their methods of coping with anger issues. Men are also known to express their anger more outwardly in more aggressive ways than women. In terms of other gender differences, "most other such differences—ranging from memory and math ability to self-esteem, communication style, and personality traits—are on the statistically modest side, physical aggression is one of the few gender differences to show a medium or larger effect" (Eliot, n.d.).

Even if you were raised in a nurturing society where you could share your emotions, the pressure that is felt internally can be enough to make you feel as though you should feel bad or guilty about your emotional state. Anger is often used as a way to mask other painful feelings that are hard to deal with and,as we discussed with the fear response, anxiety and stress are certainly among them.

Envy and jealousy are also deep emotions that are very hard for men to express in a healthy way. Often more than one emotion is felt at a time, and trying to express this complexity can be difficult and frustrating. For example, an angry boyfriend who doesn't like that his girlfriend is wearing revealing clothing might be masking a deep fear that she's going to find a different partner and leave him.

Guilt and shame can also be very heavy for men to deal with, and this can be manifested into anger. Having any emotion, especially one deemed "weak," can make a man feel shameful, exacerbating initial feelings of anger.

Other emotions that are masked by anger include loneliness, emasculation, and general physical pain. It's important to recognize these concepts about men with anger issues so that you can start to heal yourself internally.

Common Versus Healthy

It's easy to feel like you are just born this way or that as a man you are going to be angry your entire life. However, it's important to remember that just because it's normal for men to display anger issues, that does not mean that it is healthy.

Men are over three times more likely to die of suicide than women (*Suicide Statistics*, 2022). Men are the ones who are responsible for the most violent crime (*Gender and Crime*, n.d.). While this statistic is true for a multitude of reasons aside from just men's relationship with anger (like women being less likely to be arrested or convicted), it serves as a reminder that the relationship is complex, nonetheless.

It begs the question, just because something is common, does that mean it is good? "Normal" should not be directly correlated with healthy. Anger is normal, of course, that's true for everybody. But expressing it in violent and aggressive ways is also common. That does not mean that it is healthy or productive.

This is another reason why it might be hard for men to overcome their anger issues. Because it is so normalized in our society, you might fear being the one to step outside of the norm. It feels awkward and uncomfortable, and a lot of other men might even react poorly if they see you managing your anger. This type of behavior is also validated by those around us, and controlling your own emotions just might cause someone else to reflect on how they're managing their own.

Despite the fear of change, it's important that you protect your peace and do what is best for your emotional well-being.

Types of Anger

Because anger is so ubiquitous, that also means it comes in all shapes and sizes. If you learn to identify the type of anger that you experience and express, it can help you come up with more effective ways of mediating your emotions.

Most anger can be categorized into three groups (Ohwovoriole, 2021):

- passive aggressive
- aggressive
- assertive

Passive Aggressive

The first is passive aggressive. This is when there is clearly anger, but it is not being expressed in a direct way. If somebody says, "Do you want to eat spaghetti tonight?" A classic angry response might be something like, "I hate spaghetti, it's terrible when you make it." A passive-aggressive response might be, "I mean, I guess we can eat spaghetti again if that's what you want."

Passive aggressiveness is when the issue is not directly addressed and is instead repressed. This creates a multitude of issues because not only is the core issue ignored, but it's also reproducing into other little conflicts that create a very tense environment. When it comes time to finally address the core issue, you also then have to address all of the other issues brought on, making the original situation 10 times worse. On top of this, anger has time to simmer and build over time. This can sometimes be even worse.

For example, let's say that you're married, and your wife decides to bring some work friends over after work. You wanted a quiet night in, and now you have to socialize, and this makes you incredibly angry. Instead of saying anything, you keep to yourself. You fester in your room all night and think about how much your wife disrespects you and how she doesn't care about your time or emotions.

The next day, she doesn't do the dishes after dinner even though you cleaned the entire house the day before. You let this build up, and now you have two things in your mind that are leading you to prove how your wife disrespects you and your time.

Over the next two weeks, you notice every little thing she does, and you start building this case against her. Eventually, you snap, and it leads to an explosive argument. She's apologetic, but it's too late; so much time has passed that now you see her in a different light.

What could have happened instead is that you could have pulled her aside and said that you didn't want company over. She could apologize and tell you that she'll wrap it up quickly, and the next night you two can enjoy a nice dinner together. Maybe during this dinner, you even share that you had felt a little disrespected, and she apologizes and says she'll make sure to ask in the future, ensuring this issue, along with many others, is avoided. Less of your energy over the next two weeks is spent on festering and getting more angry, and instead, that energy can be put towards building your communication skills and repairing your relationship.

Those who are passive-aggressive are often trying to show some emotional control, but they're misdirecting it in a way that only makes the issues even worse.

Aggressive

The next type of anger is the aggressive type. This is direct anger. This is an unhappy customer yelling at the cashier at a fast-food restaurant because they forgot their extra burger. This is a parent screaming at their child because they aren't doing well enough on the sports team. In the example we used in the previous section, this type of anger would look like yelling at your wife or being rude to the guests, displaying your anger immediately, and being motivated by slight rage.

Aggressive anger is usually more easily identifiable, but it can sometimes be harder to control. Think of your emotions like a house. While passive-aggressive anger is kind of like mold growing where you don't see the issue until it's too late, aggressive anger would be a tree falling on your roof and causing wreckage.

Aggression is often used as a way to show control over your surroundings. If you are feeling emotionally out of control, punching a wall or tossing around items can make you feel like you have more power in the situation.

Unfortunately, aggression can cause damage, and it doesn't even fix the issue. It provides a temporary release, but it usually creates new issues. Responding to anger with aggression can make your anger heightened, and it can create a pattern of association so that you consistently respond with more and more aggression.

The best way to control this method of anger is to stop and wait before responding to this emotion. If it were as easy as this, a lot fewer people would have anger issues. We'll discuss methods of how-to best practice this later on, but for now, let's get into the last main category of anger, which is assertive anger.

Assertive Anger

Finally, the third type of general anger is assertive anger. This is when anger is expressed in a healthy way. If you're a parent who is angry with your child who keeps coming home late at night, you might sit them down and have a real conversation about the dangers that are presented to teenagers and why this is hard for you to manage. A passive-aggressive response would be withholding their privileges unrelated to their curfew, and aggression would be yelling and reprimanding them with heightened anger.

If you're unhappy because your spouse hasn't been cleaning the house enough, assertive anger would involve mimicking the behavior that you want them to have while also explaining your feelings and focusing on your personal perspective. If you express your emotions in a healthy way, it will make the situation so much better, not just in that moment, but also in future situations. Again, it's all about recognizing unhealthy patterns and then finding a way to redirect your energy to create healthier ones. Once you figure out where most of your aggression is lying, whether it's passive or active, you can break your anger down even further to help you get closer to the root of the problem.

Further Categories of Anger

The goal is to create a relationship with anger where you are assertive and can use the emotion to get what you want in a healthy and productive way. To help you do this better, let's break anger down into even smaller categories.

In a general sense, you might be feeling chronic anger. This is when anger is usually your first response. Sudden changes, whether it's a change in your location or the plans that you have for the day, might cause you to react with anger first, even though the situation ends up being fine in the end. Chronic anger is when loud noises and small minor inconveniences cause you to immediately blow up. Think about someone who might explode at a TV when a streaming service freezes or someone who yells at the service worker when their favorite dish is out of stock.

This type of anger usually manifests because you are not dealing with most of your emotions, and you're letting them become larger than the initial issue. There might also be a general stressor in your life that is taking your focus away and making it harder for you to have emotional management.

A more complex type of anger to understand is being overwhelmed or frustrated. This is often a more passive anger, and you might not react aggressively to it. However, it is still an emotion tied to anger and something that can be resolved when we look at the root of the things that are making us feel overwhelmed or frustrated.

Anger is often a reaction to people crossing our boundaries or "stepping on your toes," so to speak. On the one hand, this might deal with a lack of confidence or security. If somebody you know calls you out in front of your boss for showing up late one day, you might respond with anger. This might show in passive-aggressive behavior in the breakroom between the two of you. Alternatively, you might react aggressively by creating a plan of revenge to make them look bad in front of the boss.

When you let anger get the best of you in a situation like this, you might be struggling with some self-esteem issues in that department. If you are secure in your job and know that you don't have to worry about their snide remarks, you can let it go. You can also display assertive anger by talking this out with your coworker, but we can't always control how these interactions go. Some people aren't willing to be as in tune with their emotions as you might, and certain discussions can feel futile.

However, even when the other person is in the wrong, or you believe that they have done something bad to you, it is still up to you to control your emotional response. Though you might simply be dealing with somebody who keeps pushing your boundaries and pressing your buttons, responding with anger would still be something within your control. There will be situations where people cross your boundaries or try to intentionally get a reaction out of you. In situations like this, it can be hard to control your anger because the other person is doing something wrong. However, that doesn't mean that you have to respond in an angry way. Two wrongs don’t make a right, and, in the end, your anger will hurt you more than anyone else.

Just as there are many different types of anger, there are many ways to express your anger. Once you start to make a habit of identifying how you're feeling and how that's affecting your surroundings, it's easier to look at the ways that you are coping with this anger and expressing it. We'll get further into emotional regulation and expression later in the book, but it's important to note now how your type of anger relates to the way that you express that anger.

Why do I Need to Manage My Anger?

Have you ever been moved or inspired by art? Maybe there is a song that makes you emotional or a movie that always pulls at your heartstrings. The thing about these situations is that it can be hard to fully understand the feelings behind the emotional response. We don’t always have to investigate these feelings either; sometimes, you can simply like what you like without having to think about it. Now, if that emotion was causing you to ruin your life, damage relationships with others, or lose out on opportunities, your attitude around investigating this emotion might change.

You would want to try to understand that emotion at the core, right? That’s what we have to do with anger. It’s not the feeling that is affecting our lives but how we are using the emotional energy attached to anger.

In one study, one in five people stated that they ended a friendship with someone because of their anger issues (Anger Statistics, n.d.). 28% of people said that they are afraid of their own anger management issues (Anger Statistics, n.d.).

Anger is incredibly important for men to manage because, as we discussed in a previous section, despite men and women often feeling anger as frequently as one another, men are responsible for most violent crime (Martin, 2021).

According to the FBI (2012), men are responsible for:

- 88% of murder and non-negligent manslaughter.
- 77% of aggravated assault.
- 80% of arson as a violent crime.
- 73% of offenses against family and children.

Men are also responsible for 99% of forcible rape (FBI, 2012). Other factors play into these statistics, like how men are twice as likely to be convicted of a crime (Kelsh, 2015). Judges and law enforcement officers are more lenient on women, both consciously and subconsciously. In addition, much sexual abuse and rape goes unreported by both genders, but males are even less likely to report these instances (Jones, 2020).

Despite other factors in play, the scale is still heavily tipped towards men being large contributors to violent crime.

So, why do you need anger management? These statistics show that anger is ruining men's lives.

Of course, it needs to be emphasized that the victims are the ones who suffer the most in any crime. However, it is also true that when a man is convicted of a crime and sentenced to long prison terms, it ruins his life and his family's as well. Though men are more likely to commit crimes, they are also more likely to be victims of certain crimes, like murder (Gerster, 2020).

On a small scale, where is your aggression going? If you are a seemingly peaceful person on the outside, that aggression might be wearing down on you internally. This can lead to self-harm or other unhealthy habits.

There are many benefits to managing your anger. You will be able to increase your focus. Anger doesn't just occur at the moment that it's triggered. You can get angry over and over again by repeating the scenario in your head. Every ounce of energy that you put into anger is an ounce that is taken away from something with more meaning, like your family, friends, or career.

Your judgment will get better as you start to manage anger. Studies show time and time again that anger decreases your ability to make sound judgments (Lerner & et. al).

Your health will start to improve, you'll have more energy, and your relationships will improve. Every way that anger has negatively impacted your life creates a door that leads down a different path of beauty if you're willing to make the changes.

Your work will become more enjoyable, as will all things in life. When you start to let go of anger, you free yourself from years of damaging emotions.

Anger can't be suppressed - it has to be felt! An easy metaphor to help you understand this is that you cannot stop the rain, so you have to get used to wearing a raincoat. Trying to ignore anger will only make it fester. Most importantly, mismanaging anger can have detrimental effects on your emotional, physical, and social health.

CHAPTER 2:

Impact Of Anger on Emotional and Physical Health

The feeling of anger isn’t something that needs to be taught. Most of us are able to relate to the feelings brought on by last-minute changes to plans, having to wait longer than expected, or not being able to get what we want.

Anger is felt first in the brain, but on a much deeper level, it starts to impact our physical health. As we discussed in the last chapter, there is a chemical reaction in your body when you are stressed out. This is a good thing because it ensures that you are safe from danger.

If you are constantly firing off these hormones within your body, however, it will start to wreak havoc on every part of your anatomy. Your health is all tied together. Because your body is a machine, when one part isn’t working right, it can negatively impact the rest of the operative parts.

Where do you feel pain? You might struggle with getting jaw aches or headaches. You might have tense shoulders and a sore neck. Beyond this, your anger might start to affect the way that you sleep. You might have trouble falling asleep at night, or perhaps it's difficult for you to wake up in the morning. This starts to affect the way that you're eating as well, and before you know it, you feel as though your body is shutting down on you. Anything that affects your physical health puts you at risk for more illnesses. It can weaken your immune system, and it can make you feel as though you are sick and struggling.

When your health starts to go, your social life can also start to deteriorate. If you're not feeling like the best version of yourself, it can start to impact your personal relationships, your marriage, or even your ability to parent.

Once you start to realize all of the ways that anger has a negative effect on your life, it will be easier to be mindful of your anger. For example, if you are struggling to eat and you don't feel very hungry, you might ask yourself first, "Have I been stressed out lately?" If you're struggling to fall asleep at night, you can be mindful of the things that are keeping you awake and try to find a coping mechanism to manage this stream of thoughts. If you are feeling really tense and your shoulders are sore, it can be more comforting to know that it's related to your anxiety and your emotions, rather than believing there's not something that's more seriously wrong with you. Noticing the way that anger has a grip on your life will make it easier for you to free yourself from these symptoms.

Emotional Health

Sigmund Freud operated with the belief that depression was anger turned inwards (Cuncic, 2022). One of the first things you might notice when dealing with excessive anger issues is that you are struggling with depression.

The neurochemicals of your brain can become imbalanced with excessive anger (Cuncic, 2022). Anger can cloud our worldview, and when one thing sets you off, it's hard not to start highlighting the bad in everything else that is around you.

Anxiety

Physical health may be negatively impacted by continually activating the sympathetic nervous system's fight, flight, or freeze response, leading to stress on the rest of the body's systems (*Aspects of Anger*, n.d.).

When you have increased anger in your life, it will increase your overall anxiety. If you are somebody who is constantly getting yourself into situations involving road rage and other drivers are always setting you off, then you're going to be more aware of the "annoying" behaviors of other drivers. You're going to look at other cars and vehicles on the road, and your first thought is going to be negative. If you're in this tense state of mind, then if something minor does happen, like a car passing you on the highway, it might set you off even easier, creating a ripple effect of negative emotions. Anger can create this false sense that everyone around you is against you. Before you know it, you will feel like you're constantly battling with other drivers on the road.

When you're angry about one thing, it makes it harder to be patient with other things in your life. For example, if work is stressing you out and you're having a lot of conflicts with your co-workers, you might take that aggression home. You have to clock out every day, but that doesn't mean that your emotions are going to clock out at the same time. If you take this emotional state home with you, your family can pick up on it, and that can start to affect their emotional state as well. If dad is always coming home in a bad mood, grumpy, and angry, they're going to start to feel your emotions and have various reactions to them. This might cause them to feel more anxious and angrier as well, or they might withdraw. Even if you come home in a good mood, they might still participate in these behaviors themselves because of the expectations created from the other days.

Emotions are almost contagious in a way, especially when you have people looking up to you, like your children or your employees. This overall increased anxiety makes life feel exhausting. It starts to take away from the things that you actually enjoy, and it makes the things that you don't like feel even worse. When you are constantly stressed out and always feel this type of anxiety, it can make you feel depressed.

Depression

Have you ever found yourself saying things like this:

- What is the point of getting out of bed in the morning when everything is stressful?
- Will I ever have control over my anger?
- Why do I have to deal with such frustrating things?

Overwhelming thoughts like these can feel impossible to get over, making you feel stuck in a place of repeated misery and frustration. When you see the world as an angry and rage-filled place, it makes life feel less worth living.

Mental illness can be attributed to a chemical imbalance in your brain. When your brain is constantly firing off different neurochemicals in response to anger, it takes away important resources from other parts of the body (Anger - how it affects people, n.d.).

Being stressed out can deprive your brain of serotonin (*Serotonin Levels Affect The Brain's Response To Anger*, 2011). If you're low on serotonin, that can actually make you even more prone to anger. Not to mention that eating can make things even worse (Serotonin levels affect the brain's response to anger, 2011). If you're hungry, depressed, and stressed, it's hard not to be angry.

If you're depressed, you are also more likely to choose things that will exacerbate the problem. For example, you might start isolating yourself instead of exercising. You might start eating more instantly rewarding foods like fast foods or junk food rather than taking the time to plan and cook homemade healthier meals.

When you're stressed out, your body is going to try to level out those hormones, so it's going to seek something that gives it a good feeling, like a dopamine rush from sugar (WebMD, 2022). This might also be something like alcohol or sex. Sugar, alcohol, and sex aren't bad on a normal level, but if you're always stressed, you might always be seeking these things, and that can lead to addiction. This could also be something as simple as pulling out your phone to play a game or scroll the internet when you're stressed at work.

Whenever you feel bad, whether it's anger, anxiety, or depression, it's normal for your brain to want instant gratification. If you have a lot of work to do, the best thing to do is simply get the work done and be happy with your accomplishments. This will give you a great reward, but getting there means putting in the actual work and having to wait a day or two to see results. Instead, you can pull out your phone and watch videos of funny cats for ten minutes and feel instantly rewarded. When your body is tired from keeping up with all the stress, it's going to go for the easiest option, creating an endless, vicious cycle.

Coping Mechanisms

Cycles of mental health can create habits that are hard to break, which can affect every area of your life. You might find yourself struggling with binge eating snacks late at night during moments when you're stressed. Overeating can not only make us feel sick in the moment, but it could lead to long-term health issues like diabetes, hypoglycemia, or heart disease (Preiato, 2020).

You might be seeking sex in risky situations or participating in unprotected sex. If you have one partner, you might find that anger can still have an impact on your sex life. Pressuring partners into sex can make them feel less comfortable around you, which can hurt other areas of your relationship. You might also find that it's hard to get aroused or maintain an erection because of excess anger (WebMD, 2021). Pornography also provides instant gratification but can become addictive, leading to many other issues in your life.

Alcohol is also an easily accessible release for many, and you might find yourself struggling with this or other substances. Not only can alcohol addiction have many negative effects on your health, but it can also lead to impulsive behavior, opening up doors to other addictions.

As you can see, all of this can start to compound on itself. It clouds your thinking, and it makes you feel like you don't have a sense of control over your life. When you feel like you don't have any power over your actions or the things that happened to you, you might start seeking control in other areas. For example, if you feel like your work life is out of control, you might start to search for power within your relationships at home. If you're not getting your way, you might snap and be more likely to get into a heated argument with the people around you.

Anger is a recycled pattern that repeatedly wears us down. It chips away time and time again. That doesn't mean that you can't rebuild yourself back to who you used to be. Anger can help you emotionally. It's like a tool that will give you the ability to be mindful of what you're feeling. If you know how to use this tool to rebuild yourself rather than break yourself apart, you will be able to maintain emotional control and get back to a healthy state of mind.

Physical Health

When you think of a vision of health, what comes to mind? Likely someone who is athletic, physically fit, and coordinated. Unfortunately, this isn't always the case. Consider runners and professional athletes who suffer from heart attacks. While exercise and eating healthy are important for physical health, it's also crucial that we maintain our emotional health before it starts to chip away at our bodies. Let's look at the way anger can negatively impact your health so that you can fully comprehend just how important it is for you to manage your anger.

Cardiovascular System

Our heart is responsible for making sure that blood gets to every part of our body. When you feel excessive stress, anxiety, outside pressure, and especially anger, it will increase your heart rate throughout the day. You can be sitting on the couch under a blanket with a candlelit and a cozy movie playing in the background and still have your heart start racing. Anything that is going to negatively affect your heart rate can start to have an impact on your entire cardiovascular system. This can start by increasing your blood pressure, which leads to a host of other issues, like vision problems (American Heart Association, 2022). Outbursts and even internalized emotions are associated with a higher risk of having a heart attack or a stroke. These aren't death sentences necessarily, but they can be life-altering, especially if you experience paralysis or speech loss.

As you start to impact your body physically, it's going to make it even harder for you to have emotional management.

Anger isn't bad for your health in general; it's a natural emotion and feeling stressed about these health issues will only make things worse. Getting your heart pumping is important. That's why we need cardio exercises like jogging, dancing, walking, or swimming. Once you raise your heart rate and get your blood pumping, it increases circulation and is good for your overall health. The important thing to note is that excess anger will build on top of itself and has the potential to manifest into many different health issues.

Inflammation

Every time your body has a bruise or a cut, what happens? If you bump your knee really hard, it might swell up and get bright pink. If your cat scratches your arm, it might swell up and look dark red. When your body reacts to physical pain, it triggers your white blood cells to go to that area and fight off potential infection. This is inflammation. This is a good thing for cuts and bruises and even some parts of our body internally.

However, when you are constantly creating that chemical reaction that follows anger, this releases a higher amount of cortisol, which is harder for your body to process. Before you know it, your entire body can become inflamed in various places. Not only is this going to be painful, but constant inflammation can lead to chronic illnesses (Strong, 2015). Chronic illnesses can lead to more serious diseases or even cancer. As you can see, not one angry outburst is going to kill you, but instead, each time we lose control over our emotions, it becomes a drop in the bucket of your health. When that bucket overflows, it's going to have life-altering effects that you cannot come back from.

Gastrointestinal Issues

Some stress hormones like cortisol can affect your stomach health. If you notice that you're stressed out all the time, you might start to get stomach cramps. This might make it hard for you to eat or make the actual eating process even more painful. You might find yourself going through bouts of nausea. You might wake up in the morning and experience a gagging feeling, or you might notice that when you do sit down to eat, just taking that first bite can hurt your stomach. You then avoid eating nutritious meals because you don't have an appetite.

Stress can make it harder to tolerate certain foods, and you might find yourself struggling with things like acid reflux or heartburn (Golen, 2022). When you struggle with these things, it can make you more sensitive to certain foods, which can limit your diet. Excessive stomach acid could lead to a stomach ulcer or even damage your teeth.

Physical Pain

On top of the major health issues we discussed, being angry simply doesn’t feel good physically. When you’re stressed out, and your muscles are tense, it can make you feel weak and tired after you finally calm down.

Throughout the day, you might find that your neck and shoulders tense up and get sore or ache. You might also experience frequent tension headaches or migraines.

When you're feeling angry, you might notice that your mouth gets dry or your throat gets sore. The actions that follow anger, such as yelling, can also make us feel worse. If you cry, you can likely relate to how bouts of crying make you feel dehydrated or give you a headache. You might start to feel chest pain and tightness in your sternum because of the way that you're holding your body.

This kind of chest pain can be very scary because it makes us think we're having a heart attack or something more serious is going on with our cardiovascular system. In reality, it could simply be your muscles and the way that you're tensing them. Having the fear that something worse is going on with your health is only going to make your anxiety increase, making it even harder for you to manage your anger.

When you're stressed, tense, and your body is rigid, you might be more sensitive to pulling a muscle or straining something. For example, if you're angry with somebody and you stand up really quickly, you might feel a sharp pain in your back. If you look to your left or right really fast, you might experience pain or soreness in your neck.

Aside from your physical health, your social health is also affected. Before moving on to that aspect. It's important to see how all these things start to connect. Your emotional, physical, and social health create a triad for how you feel on a day-to-day basis. When all three of these things are healthy, it makes life easier and more enjoyable. If any one of these areas is lacking, it's going to pull the other two down as well. If you're stressed out, you might look to alcohol for an emotional release, only for it to lead to cirrhosis of the liver. If you're struggling with constant back pain, it can make you feel depressed.

Your physical or emotional health can also be harmed in a social setting. If you find yourself violently fighting with other people, you could get hurt. If you're somebody who's angry and reactive and you get into bar fights, there might be one time when somebody actually kills you. You never know if your anger is going to trigger somebody else. Even if you think that you're a stronger person, you never know what is going to happen. Anger gives you a false sense that you have control, but in reality, it could be the very thing that leads to your demise.

Recognizing the way that all of these aspects intermingle with each other will help you emphasize managing your anger so that you can take back control of your health.

Social Health

Frank P. McMurray is a 50-year-old man. The last time he was a free man was in 1994. Just 17 days after his 21st birthday, he was sentenced to life in prison after killing Mario Olivio at a red light. For almost 30 years, he has served time in prison over an angry moment (McMurray, 2022).

The thing is, this didn't all happen at once. All it took was a split second to take a life, but the time that it took to get to such an emotional place was built on years of mismanaged anger.

Situations like this happen all the time, and it's always just as devastating as the last. Don't let yourself become another statistic. Looking at all the ways that anger hurts your social health can help you finally see the big picture of just how crucial anger management really is.

Loneliness

Sometimes, being alone is nice. It's always great to wake up and have the house to yourself or to enjoy a movie when you're alone at night. However, most of us understand that being lonely all the time doesn't feel great. If you don't have a strong support system in your life, it can make getting through the day a lot harder. On top of that, it's always nice to have people that you can trust and that you love around when you need them. Birthdays, holidays, and even just weekends are so much more fulfilling when you have friends or family that you can share them with. Unfortunately, anger can get in the way of us achieving this very normal and healthy part of life.

On the surface level, this can result in the loss of some of your relationships. Look at your romantic relationships, your friendships, and the relationships that you share with family members. Have any of these ever struggled because of your or the other person's anger?

When you are close with somebody, you feel more comfortable around them. Because of this, it's easier to open up and to not hold back with some of the things that you want to say. Unfortunately, when this comfortability is mixed with anger, it makes that type of emotional freedom a little bit messier. You might find yourself snapping and bickering with your romantic partner. You might not be afraid to show your emotions around your family, resulting in screaming matches or times when objects are thrown at one another.

While relationships can be complicated, when things escalate into verbal abuse or physical violence, it can have long-lasting effects. Even if you get to a place in your life where you are not an angry person and you have control over your emotions, other people might not be as forgiving. Once you break trust, it's incredibly hard to build it back again.

If you emotionally hurt somebody, that can also trigger them to hurt themselves. You aren't responsible for anybody else's actions or what they choose to do with their life. However, you can have an influence over their thoughts and emotions, and you don't want to be somebody who is responsible for someone else's trauma. This is why it's so important to manage your social health now before it's too late.

Physical Violence

Beyond emotional abuse, physical violence can be even more damaging in certain situations. Not only are you hurting the other person, but you are also risking getting hurt in retaliation or losing your freedom.

In a study of prisoners in select Illinois and Missouri prisons, 93% of impulsive murders committed were done by people who were intoxicated or cognitively impaired at the time of the crime (White, 2013). This tells us that violent crime isn’t always carefully planned and calculated. A lot of it is based on emotion, and it is often fueled by an external substance. While you might feel level-headed and in control of your anger when sober, it's hard to say what can happen when you're impaired.

Whether you punch, kick, or hit somebody with an object, you don't know how serious the effects are going to be. Everybody might walk away with a black eye, but you never know if somebody is going to get a concussion or land badly when they fall. The point is, having a mentality of "I could never do that to someone" doesn't matter because many people who committed violent crimes probably thought that themselves at some point. Instead, it's important to have the confidence that you have control over your emotions so that they never turn physical again.

If you are somebody who has hurt someone else in the past, that doesn't mean that you can't move on. That doesn't mean that you are an evil person, and it doesn't mean that you are incapable of building strong relationships, even with the people that you've hurt. However, it is important to fully grasp the severity of physically hurting somebody else.

Any type of violence inflicted on others can lead to legal trouble for you, and even if you don't have to serve prison time, lawyer fees can be very expensive. You don't want to risk your freedom, time, or money just for a moment of anger. Aside from just hurting other people, all of these actions are also going to hurt you, sometimes even more so. After all is said and done, living with the guilt, shame, or embarrassment brought on by angry moments can be hard for anyone to manage.

In fits of anger or passionate times, you might have had moments where you destroyed property, broke things, threw objects, tore things off the wall, or punched a hole in the wall. Replacing property can not only be expensive, but it can be embarrassing to have to apologize and face the other person whose property you destroyed. Now is the time to get control of your anger so that it stops controlling your life. We never know what's going to happen in the future, but if you practice emotionally managing your fear and aggression, you can at least be assured that you can protect your own safety.

CHAPTER 3:

Emotional Intelligence

At this point in our discussion of anger, you understand that there is so much weighing on your emotions. While it might feel like anger comes naturally to you without having to put much thought into it, your emotions can be controlled in a way that provides your life with value.

Right now, can you think of something beneficial that could come to you in the future after you have an angry outburst? What positive or added benefit would come into your life if you express your anger in a violent or aggressive way? It might be hard for you to think of the benefits of rage at a time when you're peaceful, but in the moment, it can feel like expressing your anger is the most important thing to do. Has anger given you power over other people? Have you been able to use anger to control others? It's hard to think of a situation where unmanaged anger is beneficial to our health.

It's easy enough to say that you need to learn how to manage your emotions. Most of us already know this truth, and that's why you might have come here in the first place. Now it's time to recognize how you can become more aware of your anger, and understand it, and all your other emotions, on a deeper level. If you can recognize all of the little symptoms that come along with your mismanaged emotions, it makes it easier to figure out how to improve your life. If you're struggling to get sleep and you have poor eating habits, you can start by tracing these habits back to your thoughts and then back to your emotions.

So, the question still remains, how are we able to do that? Now it is time to create a mindset of awareness around anger in order to get ahead of the feelings that it can bring on.

Naming Your Emotions

The first step of emotional awareness is identifying anger when it arises. Studies show that labeling your emotions can make them easier to manage (Miller, n.d.). For example, one study tested how four different groups responded to a spider:

The first group blatantly labeled and stated their fear.

The second group responded by stating they weren't afraid of the spider.

The third said something unrelated to the spider.

The fourth group stayed silent.

One week later, it was shown that the first group felt less afraid of the spider than the others. Why does this work? When you label your fear, you turn it into something more understandable than the initial feelings it brought on (Miller, n.d.).

The first step of emotional awareness is identifying anger when it arises. To help you better understand this concept, reflect on a moment in the past when you were angry. Just let the first thought pop into your mind. When you were angry at that moment, were you able to feel it? At what point did you realize that you were actually experiencing anger? Did you have regrets about how you acted after you became aware of these emotions? For example, let's say that you got in a fight with your friend because they haven't been hanging out with you enough or giving you enough of their time. You felt like they were disrespecting you by not deciding to hang out with you. You might have lashed out at them and used hurtful words, like calling them a bad friend or selfish. Later on, maybe you realized it was mean to call them these things and that you could have expressed your emotions in a way that helped your relationship. Instead, you ended up hurting the relationship.

In this situation, you were able to gain a better sense of how you were actually feeling and how that behavior manifested itself in your and your friend's conversation. Once you're able to gain a realization of how you felt, that's when the feelings of shame or regret start to come in. Even after you apologize, it can still have damaging effects on your relationship in the future.

The point of bringing awareness around your emotions is to enable yourself to have this realization at the time of your anger. If you're able to do this, you can prevent yourself from reacting.

In that example situation, if you noticed right away that you were feeling hurt and neglected by your friend, you could have walked away from the conversation. You could have taken some time to cool off, and once you were level-headed, you could have returned to the conversation and explained the reasons you were feeling hurt.

By taking a moment away to be mindful of your feelings, you make yourself more aware of your emotions so that they have less of an impact on your mental and physical state. When anger is managed, you are able to ensure that you don't make your relationship with your friend any worse. You are also able to grasp how your emotions are affecting your thoughts, and you can share that with your friend so that you can build and flourish the relationship.

Once you open up, the other person is also more likely to share where they're coming from. Your friend might be able to let you know a little bit more about why they've been so distant. Maybe they're going through something difficult and want to be alone, and that allows you to have empathy for their situation while they also build empathy for yours.

Emotional Labels

The first step in understanding your feelings is naming them. Acknowledge that anger exists. You don't have to hide from it, and you don't have to try and pretend like you're fine when you're not. It's exhausting, and it only makes things worse.

One of the most effective tools for naming your emotions is familiarizing yourself with an emotion wheel. This wheel typically lists 3-6 core emotions surrounded by another circle of more detailed emotions.

To help introduce you to the subject, visualize a common food. We've all had it before: a pizza. Imagine that the pizza is cut into six individual slices. One slice is sadness. Let's say this is your favorite pizza. Pick 2-3 toppings. All of these individual toppings represent an even more detailed description of that emotion. These might be feelings like:

- loneliness
- regret
- remorse
- grief
- embarrassment
- disappointment

Sadness can be a very complex emotion. Each of these subcategories offer different feelings along with different coping mechanisms. Learning how to differentiate these complex emotions will give you more power over knowing how to handle them as they come on.

The next slice is anger. The toppings on this slice represent:

- frustration
- disrespect
- withdrawal

How does your anger feel? How can you describe your anger without using the actual word? Are you annoyed? Are you enraged? Are you slightly baffled? There's a large range of how your anger appears in your life, and naming the different variances will help you manage the feelings that are attached to this.

The next slice is fear. The toppings on this might be:

- helplessness
- rejection
- anxiety

You might just be slightly spooked. Maybe it's late at night, and you hear a weird noise downstairs. In a more intense example, perhaps your loved one is getting surgery, and you're absolutely terrified, and there's nothing that seems like it could alleviate your feelings right now. Fear, anger, and sadness represent a large range of "negative" emotions. This doesn't mean they are bad, but instead, the feelings and situations they are attached to are commonly undesirable. The range from positive to negative can help you recognize the balance in your emotions. Sometimes we identify just our negative emotions, and we focus on those without recognizing what it feels like to actually have those positive emotions as well.

Let's move on to the more positive side of the emotion wheel. Think about the slice of happiness. This is such a broad category, and it's usually the piece that we want the most. This piece has the most toppings on it. It doesn't have any of those extra bubbles or patches where there isn't enough cheese. It's a picture-perfect slice and the one everyone reaches for when the pizza box opens. Happiness is:

- joy
- hopefulness
- energized
- enthused
- mesmerized
- ecstatic
- relieved
- grateful

The fifth slice is surprise. This is a slice that can actually be both good and bad. This includes emotions like:

- shocked
- confused
- startled

You might be excited. This is something like a surprise on your birthday or for an anniversary. Alternatively, you might be confused. Somebody might have just given you news that you don't really want to hear or that you didn't expect. You might be uncertain. Sometimes you simply are not sure how you're feeling, and even that itself can be an emotion that you identify with. Recognizing that you're uncertain shouldn't put pressure on you, but instead, it should help create an air of awareness so that as you process your thoughts and feelings, you stay focused on naming your emotion.

Finally, the last slice is calm. Calm emotions can further be broken down into feelings such as:

- tranquility

- peace
- comforted
- secure

This can be almost a feeling of neutrality. This might be when you're peaceful or comfortable. When you're calm, you sometimes are confident. You know exactly what you need to do. You're not afraid to step up and take leadership, and you are prepared for anything that comes your way.

Continually recognizing and naming your emotions familiarizes you with everything that passes through your brain. This will help you not only enjoy the good emotions even more, but it will help you manage the ones that have a negative impact on your life.

You don't have to use the pizza visualization either. Think of something circular. If you're into cars, maybe it's a tire. If you have more of a sweet tooth, maybe it's a pie. Break your emotions down into 3-6 main categories, and then reflect on the deeper descriptions within each category to help you start the journey of emotional awareness.

Understanding Your Emotions

Emotions can be scary and hard to manage, so you might have spent a large portion of your life ignoring them. Now it is time to shine the light directly on your feelings. Face them head-on and look them right in the eyes, and you will see they are not as scary as you think. The next level up is developing emotional intelligence.

Now that you know the name of your emotions, it's time to get to know them on a deeper level. Picture all of your emotions as people. Let's say you're at a business meeting or a conference, and you're getting to know everybody. You learn their names, and you can recognize them when they walk by. Beyond that, it's time to learn who they really are. What are all the little quirks about them? What are the little hidden secrets that only you know and that only you feel?

Emotional intelligence is a tool that can be used to calm anger. It helps you create empathy and social awareness so that relationships are improved, and it gives you the ability to master your emotions. Emotional intelligence helps you not only understand yourself but also what other people are going through and what they might be feeling.

This is important on a small scale because it can help you make sense of why somebody acted a certain way or did something specific. For example, if you are somebody who struggles with road rage and other drivers make you easily upset, you can reframe the situation and use empathy to try and understand what the driver is going through. Maybe they are late for work, and they're in a rush, or maybe a family member just died, and they're struggling to stay focused. Of course, you could always argue that no matter what you're going through, you have to be safe on the road, but at the same time, trying to understand what they're going through puts our own life in perspective and can make things a bit easier. There are four parts that create someone's emotional intelligence:

- self-awareness
- empathy
- self-management
- social skills

Self-Awareness

The first step is to create self-awareness. As we discussed in the last chapter, this begins by naming your emotions. Again, it's important to recognize both positive and negative emotions so that you can familiarize yourself with how you're feeling until it becomes normal for you to maintain that level of awareness.

Beyond that, it's important to find a deeper meaning behind what your emotions are actually telling you. It's one thing to simply be mad because you got off work and you came home, and the house was a mess. On a deeper level, why does this upset you so much? Is it because it's overwhelming to look at? Is there a deeper issue going on with you and the people you're living with and how they're maintaining the space? Do you have trouble transitioning throughout your day, or do you need more time to decompress?

Awareness is all about maintaining regulation so that you stay grounded in reality. You could sit and analyze your feelings endlessly, but at a certain point, you do have to stop and decide how you are going to take action to alleviate or change these emotions.

Awareness also means recognizing what your motivations are, and why you're feeling a certain way (Tjan, 2015).

If you're upset because a friend decided to start dating a certain person, why are you angry? Are you jealous because you want a partner? Are you annoyed because you think that they have poor judgment? What is your actual motivation behind the anger? Looking at the motivation behind emotions can help you realize they aren't as big of a deal after all.

Awareness also means recognizing the things that trigger you and understanding the way that you react to them. This gives you the power to start to understand your patterns of thought, and it gives you the power to prevent them in the future.

Empathy

The second part of developing emotional intelligence is empathy. Empathy is the ability to recognize and understand the emotions of others.

Sympathy is when you feel bad for somebody. If you see a news story about a little girl who lost her father, you can feel bad for her. It must be sad for her to have to grow up without a dad. Empathy is really feeling what she's going through on a deeper level. If you actually lost a parent when you were a young child, it'll be easier for you to have empathy for her because you know exactly what that feels like. If you don't have experience with this, you can try and relate it to your own. Maybe you have a little cousin or sister. What would her life look like if she lost her dad? How would your life look different if you were in her situation? Sympathy is important, but taking empathy further can give us greater insight into everyone's emotions. Having empathy is seeing things from her perspective and visualizing what it's like to live like her. You don't just see that sad moment and move on, but instead, you think about what it's like to grow up and be a teenager and be a young woman and what she and her dad might have shared together that was special. You're actually living through her experiences when you have empathy.

Empathy also helps you understand the situations that bring people to where they are, while also accepting and embracing differences. In our current world, people can be very divided on heated topics. It's important to have strong morals and beliefs, but at the same time, having empathy helps you see the perspectives of the people that you disagree with.

Picture a hot topic that you have a strong opinion on that often divides people. You might think to yourself, "How could anybody believe the opposite of what I do?" Empathy forces you to look at your own life and see how you were taught everything that you believe today. You might have been directly taught these beliefs by your parents, or perhaps you had to go through certain experiences to learn the values that you have today. Some people might have had different parents that taught them the exact opposite. They might have also gone through their own experiences that shaped their vision and their viewpoint. If you see everybody else's life from your own perspective, it makes the world a lot more divisive.

If you think to yourself, "I can't think that way, and I don't understand why they do," it can make you feel more hatred toward them. Empathy allows you to say, "I understand what they went through. I can see why they're there in their life."

You still don't have to agree with them, but you can at least recognize the different paths your lives have taken and why the two of you might feel the pressures to uphold certain beliefs. This can help you reduce intense feelings so the two of you can have a more civil and productive conversation.

Self-Management

The third part of emotional intelligence is self-management. This is knowing how to regulate the feelings once you have them. Self-management involves being motivated to make an actual change because you can see the way that your own thoughts and actions are affecting your life.

Self-management involves being critical and having discipline but also having positivity and self-love. You should be able to recognize when you need to step things up, but you should also be your own biggest cheerleader and be able to congratulate yourself when you make accomplishments. Self-management goes both ways, so don't get it confused with self-deprecation. Self-deprecation can often make us feel like we're aware of our emotions or that we're aware of certain behaviors, but it often focuses on the negative rather than an objective standpoint.

When you have self-management, you're able to make decisions with confidence, and you're also able to adapt to any situation. Self-management also means knowing how to take those negative emotions and use them in a positive way. For example, if you feel bad about yourself and you're not getting enough work done, you can use those emotions to help motivate you to start waking up earlier and getting more accomplished.

Social Skills

The fourth part of emotional intelligence involves your social skills. This is different from empathy because it's about how you handle the situation, even after you recognize the emotions in other people. For example, let's say you get into a screaming match with your partner, they leave the house for two days, and they don't return or call to let you know where they are.

Eventually, they come home. They're extremely apologetic, and they share with you that this is how their parents used to handle conflict, and isolation is normal for them. You can be empathetic towards that and recognize that they weren't necessarily taught healthy coping mechanisms. You can accept their apology and agree to move on. But at the same time, you can also set the boundary and say that this isn't okay with you and that you won't accept that kind of behavior in the future. You can be empathetic toward someone while still disagreeing or being upset with them.

Social skills help you manage things in a healthy way while also building stronger connections with the other person. Social skills give you the ability to change other people's emotions, or at least slightly influence them.

For example, let's say you're the shift leader at a busy sandwich shop. You have five people working under you during your shift. It's Sunday morning, and everyone is really tired and lethargic. The energy is low, the store is messy, and it's starting to make you frustrated that the team isn't stepping it up. How can you use your social skills to change the situation for the better rather than letting anger lead to an outburst? You can consider changing the mood. Everyone is low energy, so what will make them happier? Maybe you buy them a dozen donuts or let them play their own music for the shift to boost morale. You might create a contest and tell them if the store gets cleaned up by a certain time, everyone can clock out 15 minutes early.

Knowing how to use your social skills is extremely beneficial not just for you but for the people around you as well. If you can learn how to increase your emotional intelligence, it will give you the ability to not only use your anger for good but to use all your emotions to get the things that you want in life.

Identify Your Thought Patterns

Once feelings turn into thoughts and we are able to easily label those, we can begin to uncover patterns. A cognitive distortion is a disordered pattern of thinking. Sometimes these are learned from our surroundings, and other times they are simply a result of anxiety. Once one disordered pattern starts, it's easier to develop more, and before you know it, your thinking and judgment are clouded by negative thoughts.

Can you think of a person who is always pessimistic? Do you know someone who is afraid of everything? When it seems like a person's personality is stuck in a certain place, they might be struggling with cognitive distortions. When we're angry, it can make us feel confident that we're right. The adrenaline and attention focused on the trigger give us a false sense of power. Anger is the result of our thoughts, and cleaning up the endless cyclones twisting throughout your brain will help you reframe any situation.

For example, emotional reasoning is often a common cognitive distortion involving anger. It makes you feel that since you are experiencing a certain thought or feeling, it must be true. This can cause you to cherry-pick "evidence" to support this.

Below are a few more different types of cognitive distortions that you might be struggling with. Identifying these patterns can help you stop the cycle and create a more realistic perspective, freeing you from negativity.

Overgeneralization

Overgeneralization occurs when we make assumptions about certain situations. If you had a bad experience at a restaurant because of a rude waiter, you might believe that the restaurant is terrible and decide to never return. If you ask a girl for her number at a club and she laughs at you, you might think all women hate you and that you'll never get a date. If you have a bad day at work and someone forgets to fulfill their duty, you might think that everyone you work with is a failure and your job is toxic. It's easy to let one small thing balloon into sweeping generalizations about reality in general.

Overgeneralization also involves the use of "absolute" phrasing. This creates a limit on your belief system, making it harder to see the real picture. Absolute phrases include:

- always/never
- best/worst
- everything/nothing

When you apply this to your belief system, it might change the way you view the world. For example, if your partner leaves their wet towel on the carpet after a shower one day, you might say, "My partner is ALWAYS making such a mess." If you get dinner delivered and they forgot your drink, you might say, "They NEVER get my order right." Absolute phrasing creates a language in your head that can be hard to break. Other common absolute phrasing includes:

- Everything sucks.

- She is the worst.
- I have nothing to do.

Repeating these things makes you more likely to believe they are true. If you notice yourself doing this, stop and focus on the singular situation. If there is a pattern, like constant rejection from women or a disorganized workspace, how can you affect this? Maybe your approach when flirting is coming off bad, and you can read some books on dating or ask a friend for advice. Maybe there's a flaw in the work system, and finding it could actually make you look good in front of your boss. Some situations will be out of our control, but if you only focus on the generalizations you made, it will be harder to create any great change at all.

Reframing the Situation

Take a second to use your hands and create a small rectangle. Hold it up to any area around you. What can you say about what you see inside the frame? Now move your hand elsewhere and describe that scene.

Any situation can be framed in multiple different ways. If you're in your bedroom, for example, you can create a frame around the dirty clothes in the corner, and then a frame around a clean end table that was recently dusted. If you only looked at the dirty clothes, you might be able to make the assumption that the room is messy. If you only saw the clean and organized end table, you could say the room is spotless. In reality, the room is fine in terms of cleanliness and could use a quick tidying up of the dirty clothes.

Our perspective, experiences, personal preferences/opinions, and core beliefs can create a 4-sided frame for how we view the world. Break the frame open and look at the entire picture.

Personalization

Have you ever walked by a group of whispering people, only to wonder if they were talking about you? You might have felt personalization. Of course, most of us, no matter how nosy we are, get a little curious when we hear people whispering. Are they talking about us? Are they talking about someone we know? Did something bad happen?

Personalization is when we insert ourselves into any situation, usually in a negative way. This can be damaging because it can give you this false sense that you have more influence than you do, adding pressure and anxiety to your thoughts. For example, let's say you went to a friend's birthday party. You're enjoying a glass of wine when a friend walks by and accidentally bumps you slightly on the shoulder. Your red wine splashes all over their cream knit sweater, and the party goes quiet. Another friend comes to the rescue and makes a magic concoction that lifts the stain. Everyone laughs it off, they tell you it's fine, and the party rages on. However, the next day, you're lying awake in bed, going over the situation in your mind. You're mortified and embarrassed, and you want to shrivel up and disappear.

You might feel this with any sort of embarrassing scenario. In reality, your friends haven't even thought about it; some drank so much wine that they forgot it even happened, and the person who actually had the wine spilled on them feels just as bad for bumping you on the shoulder.

Personalization makes us think that our thoughts and actions are more severe than they are and that other people are more greatly affected by them. When you're experiencing personalization, you're actually putting your own perspective into their thoughts and motives. If you think to yourself, "My friends hate me and are just pretending to like me," you're villainizing your friends. If they knew you were thinking this way, they might be upset. They aren't capable of faking friendship like that, so your thoughts are not only hurting you, but they're hurting the image you have of your friends.

CHAPTER 4:

Environmental Factors

While most of our emotions start internally, we can also look at our environmental factors to determine what types of situations we are in that have been triggering us. Environmental factors can have an influence on the way that we feel, and they will often add fuel to the fire that is our anger.

If you're able to identify the environmental factors that are triggering you, it will be easier to implement healthy coping mechanisms. It's important to understand the factors that cause your anger so that you can learn how to not only be prepared for the potential triggers that might arise, but also to have a plan in place that's waiting for you when the moment comes that you have to face the triggers.

If you're able to analyze the environmental factors that have been contributing to your anger, you can usually boil them down into a few core fears. Here are the five core fears that we all share, according to psychologist Karl Albrecht (2012):

- extinction
- mutilation
- abandonment
- loss of autonomy

- humiliation

When you think of fear, you can think of obvious anxieties like the fear of dying or getting hurt. Things like heights, spiders, and planes are common and can be related to our potential extinction (death) or mutilation (physical harm).

On a deeper level, some of the greatest fears we grapple with are emotional ones. If we are able to analyze what they actually mean, it will be easier to control our environmental factors or, at least, be less triggered when having to face them.

Family Environment

One of the biggest influences in your environment might be your family life. As we discussed, when talking about empathy, we all have been raised differently. Everybody comes from a different background. This includes your family structure. Were you raised by a mother and a father who are married and both had steady jobs? Were you raised by a single parent?

Were you raised by other family members, like an aunt or a grandparent? Were you in a foster care system? Were you raised by older siblings, even though your parents lived in the house with you?

On top of this, where were you raised? Did you live in a city where you had access to anything you needed? Did you live in the middle of nowhere where you had to be more self-sustaining? Did you go to a big high school with a diverse population? Did you go to a small school with less than 100 people? These types of things shape who you are and present incredibly differing experiences from person to person.

It's important to look at your past to see what triggers might have developed early on.

As Children

Those who experienced childhood trauma are more likely to be angry as adults (Upham, 2023). Studies show that when children experience something emotional, it can be harder for them to manage their feelings well into adulthood.

Past and even present family situations can be the root cause of some of your anger. Did you struggle with parental loss? This might be a parent leaving after a divorce. Perhaps you never even knew one of your parents, or maybe one of your guardians passed away at a young age.

Divorce is also common and can be very traumatic for children. Having to be placed in the middle of two parents can make managing your emotions confusing. How can you love one parent while the other is saying such negative things about them? How can you choose where to live or who to spend more time with? Seeing constant fighting between the two adults that are supposed to be your most dependable figures is very hard for children to comprehend. When your parents were in such emotional stages, it might have been harder for you to express your emotions, leading to normalcy surrounding emotional suppression.

Any type of instability at home can be very emotionally damaging to children. This can include not having security. If you struggled to know where your next meal was going to come from, or you worried that you might be evicted or lose your home, that can be very stressful for anybody to deal with, but especially a child still developing their mind.

Neglect is also a form of childhood abuse. Even if you had two parents who worked really hard, they might not have been around frequently and missed major milestones. This is common for single parents or parents who are struggling with addiction. Learning independence at an early age can be healthy, but not when you don't have any guidance. As an adult, you might maintain this belief that you can do it on your own. If you can't depend on the very people that were supposed to always be there for you, it can make it hard for you to trust anyone. When this ability to be dependent on others is gone, it will make you believe that you are incapable of receiving any help at all.

As a child, it's extremely hard to manage your emotions, even in a healthy environment. If you were never given the opportunity to learn how to control your feelings in a healthy way, it's going to be very hard to learn how to do this on your own as an adult.

You learn how to be a family unit in your childhood, so that can affect your adult relationships. For example, if you had an unstable home and you never knew where you were going to be sleeping that night, this could affect your ability to commit to serious situations as an adult. Childhood trauma isn't always black and white. Just because you experienced one thing doesn't necessarily mean that you're going to act in a certain way. However, if you bring awareness to the patterns that you went through as a kid, it can give you an outline for how to evaluate who you are as a person today.

As Adults

In addition to our past, our present situations can also affect our family environment. Are you struggling with bills? If you are the head of the household, you are the one who has to make most of the income, which can be very stressful for you. If you are dependent on somebody else's income, that can be just as stressful. Either situation can cause insecurity or resentment in certain relationships, which can fuel your anger.

Conflicts can arise in basic domestic duties. Perhaps you have a different parenting style from your partner. Maybe you and your roommates have different cleanliness habits at home. Not only are the actual situations you live with anger-inducing, but thinking about them when you're not at home can start to trigger anger.

How is your family environment, and how is this affecting the way that everybody manages their emotions? Even things that are supposed to be happy, like vacations or holidays, might be stressful when emotions aren't managed. Is there constant explosive arguing at home? Alternatively, maybe you and your family members aren't sharing enough with each other. The thing about our family environment is that it is a daily occurrence. You likely come home to your spouse every single day. If you're a parent, you have to raise your children every day (even if you have shared custody, you're likely still thinking about them when they are not around).

If you're constantly arguing, bottling up emotions, or clashing with the ones that you live with, it is going to hurt everybody involved. When referring to Dr. Albrecht's (2012) core fears, you can relate your family environment to the fear of abandonment or rejection. We are group animals, and we have a deep urge to feel accepted and embraced in our society. You can use this to look at your family life and see if any of those fears are making you an angry person. If you were abandoned as a child by a parent, it can be difficult for you to manage those feelings now, and it might even affect your parenting style.

If you witnessed unstable relationships, that could be making it hard for you to open up and connect to your partner now. Look deeply at these fears and how they're manifesting into anger so that you can learn how to control your environmental factors.

Work Environment

Another core fear is the loss of autonomy. Autonomy is your ability to have control of your life and make whatever decisions you want. It's your ability to display your free will and your strong, independent voice.

Autonomy, control, and power can all mean different things to different people.

Some people enjoy being in power, and they like having control over others. Others would rather follow and let somebody else take the lead. Regardless of where you fall, all humans want at least some form of autonomy. Even if we choose to follow others, that is still a decision we can make on our own rather than being forced to listen to someone.

Autonomy can be physical in that you want to have control over your body and be able to go where you want. Some people have fears like claustrophobia, or they can't handle being restricted in any way.

Autonomy also means being able to make your own decisions and not have anybody else tell you what to do. One thing that strips away our feeling of autonomy can be work. Even if you don't have a job, or you're not in school, you might feel the pressure to work from our society.

Unfortunately, work can also be a huge trigger for our anger. Your autonomy is even further stripped depending on what position you're in. You might have a demanding boss who takes your time even when you're not clocked in. You might have to work overtime or work two jobs just to make ends meet.

Most of us would probably lose a lot if we stopped working. Whether you would have to sell your house or get rid of your belongings, work is a requirement for many people to maintain the life that they have. This pressure itself is enough to make anyone angry, but on top of that, stressors at our actual jobs can be very rage-inducing. This might be unfairness, a lack of respect, or general unhappiness with your job.

Sometimes jobs feel like a dead end and like there's no getting out of it. The pressure to do something that you're passionate about can also distract you if you're working a job that you don't really enjoy.

The competitive nature of certain jobs can be incredibly stressful and weigh heavily on you. If you ever feel stuck or like you can't advance anymore in your career, that can be a feeling that strips you of your autonomy.

It's not necessarily that you have the desire to be the boss or be in charge of everybody else. A lot of people don't want this because they don't want the responsibility, even if it means getting paid more. At the end of the day, nobody likes to get bossed around, and most of us want to be able to take matters into our own hands and make decisions that work best for us.

Careers can also make us really reflect on our entire life. It's easy to fall in the “grass is greener on the other side" mindset. When you went to college, perhaps you started by majoring in theater, but instead, you decided to pursue pharmacy. Now as you count pills every day, you wonder what life would have been like had you decided to follow your passion as a playwright.

Alternatively, maybe you are struggling to find a job in your field, and all you can think about is how you should have tried a little bit harder in school so that you could have become a doctor.

The pressure never stops.

There is always something new to be anxious about when it comes to our work environment. The added pressure of what could happen to us if we don't work makes these things even more intense. You might be somebody who is close to homelessness or doesn't have access to food or healthcare because of their current economic standpoint.

Having this loss of control is very triggering for anger and showing anger can often be an attempt at regaining control. Unfortunately, it's a misfired attempt, and what ends up happening is that things get even worse.

If you're struggling with your work environment, it's important to look at the root causes. Are you afraid of losing your job? Are you feeling inadequate in your position? Are you suffering because you don't think you've made the right decisions thus far?

To help you manage your work environment, it's important to look for forms of stability. Do you have backup plans in place if something were to happen to your job? Can you create stronger channels of communication between you and the people that you work with so that conflicts are easier to manage? Look at these main issues so that you can find the best method of mitigating your biggest problems. We'll cover more specific coping strategies later, but for now, just like your emotional awareness, it's important to gain spatial awareness around environmental factors that trigger anger.

Society and Social Media

The last of the five core fears proposed by Dr. Albrecht is humiliation. While getting slightly embarrassed might not feel as bad as one of the other fears, like losing a limb or being abandoned by your one true love, humiliation can still cost lives. It's estimated that potentially thousands of people die every year from preventable bowel disease or treatable AIDS that could have been managed had they been able to report without being held back by feelings of shame (Fisher, n.d.).

In addition, research shows that one in three women delay seeking medical treatment because they are afraid that they're overreacting and want to avoid embarrassment (Are Women Literally Dying Of Embarrassment?, 2018). The pressures from society make us feel that we are not good enough, that we have inherent flaws, or that we should be ashamed of certain interests or behaviors.

Shame and embarrassment are even harder to speak up about as men because of the culture surrounding how we share emotions. Dealing with any type of embarrassment, humiliation, or shame can certainly be fuel to your anger.

How we are perceived by others is one thing that is often out of our control. We are social animals, so we all have this natural urge to fit into society. Unfortunately, technologies in our day and age can make it even harder to find our place.

Anyone can get online at any time and say whatever they want with little to no repercussions. You can create a fake account with a secret name and use that to be aggressive or harass others online. You might get blocked or deleted, but you can always make another account. This anonymity allows you to express anger, and while it might feel like a release, it can actually cause these emotions to follow into your offline life.

Though you might be able to compartmentalize your online persona from who you are as a person, it can still affect your patterns of thought. While you might be burying deeper emotions in your waking life, as we know by now, emotional repression can be life-threatening.

In addition, social media taps into our desire to maintain justice (Heshmat, 2018). As men, this is certainly something that we are pressured to strive for. If you are the head of your family, you have this pressure to do what is right and make sure that everyone is treated the way they deserve to be. Social media can give us this sense that we are achieving justice. You can get online at any time and get into an argument with a stranger about a topic that the two of you completely disagree on. This type of interaction can create a false sense that we are maintaining justice, but in reality, it can exacerbate aggression.

Social media makes it easier to compare our lives to others. You can see other men who have partners, cars, and houses that you desire. Your peers might share their career achievements or other impressive personal accomplishments. This type of comparison can make us feel that we don't have a sense of control over our bodies and lives, and seeking that power can lead to unhealthy coping mechanisms. For example, 1 in 4 people who suffer from eating disorders are men (Eating Disorders in Males, n.d.). Compounded on this issue is the lack of outlets for men to express their feelings, which can lead to these disordered eating habits. In addition, "men who experience physical or sexual trauma often respond by attempting to alter their bodies to become more "masculine," attempting to gain muscle to protect themselves from future victimization (Eating Disorders in Males, n.d.)."

Learning how to recognize the influence our environment has on us gives us our sense of power back. Once we've regained our sense of power, it will be easier to manage anger now and in the future.

Awareness is the most important step in anger management. This awareness is still a learning process, and it can take time to fully comprehend what your emotions are telling you. As you learn how to navigate your own brain, life will get easier. In the meantime, understanding practical strategies of anger management can ensure that you stay on the right track toward a life free from anger.

CHAPTER 5:

Strategies

What are the best methods for overcoming anger?

There are many strategies that can be used to control and manage anger. Not everything that works for some will have the same results for others. It is important, however, to at least try all of the strategies once. If you don't think it will work for you, dedicate just an hour to trying it, and you might find yourself surprised. Once something does work for you, stick to it, and you will see amazing results over time.

Short-Term Strategies

Short-term strategies are the little habits that you can implement the moment that you feel anger. This requires awareness at first, but the second that you have the realization of "I am angry," you know exactly what strategy to try next.

Think of it like physical pain. If you're somebody who struggles with back pain, in the long term, you want to go to your doctor to figure out what the root cause of the problem is. Is it a pulled muscle? Did you slip a disc? However, that takes time and might result in long periods of healing that stretch over weeks.

Though you can't treat it right away, in the immediate moment, you still want release from that back pain. You can at least alleviate some of the symptoms that come along and prevent your back pain from getting worse. These instant releases might be things like a hot shower, a soak in a hot tub, an ibuprofen, or a massage. While it doesn't cure the pain, it at least takes away some of it.

When it comes to anger, short-term strategies are like your instant pain relief.

Deep Breathing

The first thing you want to start practicing is deep breathing. When we are angry, our breathing starts to change, and our heart rate increases. All of a sudden, you might find that you're struggling to catch your breath. If you take a moment to stop and breathe, this can have extremely beneficial effects on your body. The next time you're angry, take a moment and start to breathe in through your nose and out through your mouth. One way that you can practice doing this right now is by closing your mouth and breathing in as you count to five. Hold your breath for a moment, and then breathe out through a small hole in your mouth. Repeat this for several rounds until you start to feel relaxed. You might feel slightly lightheaded or dizzy at first, but that is normal. If you feel excessive dizziness or like your heart rate starts pounding, you might need to slow your breathing.

Practice this as you keep reading.

Breathe in through your nose for one, two, three, four, and five. Hold it. Breathe out through a small hole in your mouth for five, four, three, two, one.

Feel the breath deep into your chest and let it sit in your stomach for a moment, and then breathe it out. As you are doing this, visualize yourself breathing in all of your negative emotions and all of your anger as you breathe out. Picture that anger traveling from your body and going far away from you.

As you are breathing and counting when you are angry, it helps to ensure that you are able to think before you speak. Go through your mind and try to determine what you are going to benefit from this situation. If you are able to stop and reflect on the positive outcome of managing your anger, then you will be able to control your words much easier.

Humor

To keep things light hearted, try using humor when you are angry. If you pour yourself a cup of coffee, only for it to splash on your white shirt as you take your first sip in the morning, you might say to yourself, "That's wonderful. That's exactly what I wanted to happen." Having this kind of sarcastic attitude can make things a little bit more lighthearted while still expressing some of your anger.

If somebody is really trying to rile you up and make you angry, try and laugh it off. Start with a smile. Simply smiling or even faking a laugh can make us more likely to have a genuine laugh or smile. Not only can it boost your good feelings, but it can also show the other person that you are unaffected, making them less likely to egg you on. It also gives you a chance to simply walk away. Deciding to chuckle at the situation and remove yourself makes you feel better later on, and it makes you look better to your peers around you rather than attacking the other person or fighting back.

Relaxation Spaces

It's also important to focus on having other forms of relaxation that you can use. How can you create a safe space so that when you are feeling angry, you can go directly to this spot to stop and breathe?

If you're somebody who enjoys playing video games, reading, or watching movies, you can have a special spot set up to do this when you're feeling angry. If one day you find yourself scrolling online, you can put your phone down and dive right into that activity and distract yourself. Just make sure you're not choosing a violent video game that will only increase your anger.

Consider something as simple as sitting outside and letting the sun shine down on you. Incorporate more relaxation techniques into your daily mind and have these things ready so that if you're angry, your first thought can be simply going to this place to clear your head.

If you come home from a long day of work, you can go right into your office and start reading your favorite book for thirty minutes while your mind unwinds. If you get in a fight with your partner, you can grab an ice-cold glass of water and sit on your balcony and feel the sun hit your face.

Having these relaxation spaces provides you with a safe spot to go so that when you are feeling angry, you know exactly what to do next.

Exercise

Another great strategy that can help you manage your emotions is exercise. Any form of exercise is good for your health in general, but it will also give you a distraction from your anger. Just like sleeping, eating, or feeling stressed out, moving your body is also a chemical reaction. Your heart will start beating, and you might start sweating.

Start exercising more by simply going for a walk. This is an excellent way to clear your head, especially with your favorite music playing. You can also try signing up for a gym membership so that this could be your safe space when you are feeling angry.

When exercising, you can sort your thoughts out so that if the problem still persists, you at least have a level head and can approach it with the right strategy. Exercising gives you a chance to do something with the increased heart rate and energy boost that anxiety gives you.

Support System

Another short-term method is to have a support system. Can you ask a friend to be your anger mentor so that when you are having a moment of rage or panic, you can call them?

This way, if you are triggered, and you're having an especially angry day, you can text or call that friend who understands your anger issues. If this other person has anger issues as well, this can be a way to hold each other accountable and see your similarities in a new light, making it easier to be self-reflective. Just be cautious that you aren't validating each other and making things worse. Calm friends can be just as helpful because they serve as a reminder that anxiety, fear, and anger aren't needed in that situation and that it is possible to keep your cool.

Have conversations with this person and share what your triggers and frequent coping mechanisms are. This will help give them awareness so that if you're not seeing the full picture, they have an idea of how to show that to you.

Short-term strategies are great, but beyond that, it's important to make sure that you are incorporating just as many long-term strategies. If you have the long-term strategies in place, you can manage your anger on a bigger scale so that you aren't as frequently triggered.

Long-Term Strategies

The most effective long-term strategy you will have for your anger is addressing the underlying emotions that are causing anger. That is what we have been discussing so far in this book; creating that emotional awareness and getting a better understanding of your emotions will help you be able to cognitively restructure your brain.

Anger comes naturally to you, and it can feel so out of control because it is hardwired into the patterns of your brain. Anger can be the immediate response and the default reaction to any outside stressor. Cognitive restructuring means shaping the way that your brain thinks. If you stub your toe, you might scream expletives at the top of your lungs, throw whatever you're holding, or slam doors and cabinets. Eventually, you can restructure your brain so that if you stub your toe, the first thing you do is walk away and practice deep breathing exercises.

Think of it like working out to get a new body. Picture somebody who struggles with their weight and has a body shape that they simply don't want. They then start working on strength training exercises to shape their waist, their glutes, and their chest. Eventually, their body changes. Anyone who has struggled with their weight knows that changing it can be difficult, but with dedication each day, great change will be seen down the line.

If your body is able to change drastically over the years, it's easy to see that your brain can be just as easily shaped and reformed.

As we discussed previously, some of the cognitive distortions that you're having can make it hard for you to follow down different neural pathways. What are the best long-term strategies for rewiring your brain?

Talk It Out!

It doesn't matter if it's your best friend or the notes app on your phone. Taking your feelings from your brain to the outside world helps you make more sense of them.

It might feel awkward at first if emotional sharing isn't common in certain groups in your life, but once that door opens, it usually stays open. Talk to your spouse or partner. Talk to your mom, your dad, or your grandparents. Talk to your neighbor or somebody who you look up to. You will be surprised at how many people have similar struggles to you but have just been keeping them inside.

If you have anybody in your life that you feel safe and comfortable around, share your struggles with them. It's terrifying having to say things out loud. It can feel like it almost validates them. If you say, "I'm an angry person, and I have trouble controlling my emotions," you might think that you'll feel shameful or embarrassed, but it can actually make you feel powerful. You're not afraid of sharing this anymore, and instead, the truth is out in the open.

Sharing your emotions is a way to release them. Not only is having negative emotions hard to deal with, but hiding them can be even more tiring. Sometimes simply sharing your thoughts is enough for you to realize that you don't actually feel that way, and instead, you just had a thought reoccurring in your brain. For example, you might share with your partner that you're struggling with your relationship. In your mind, you might have thought, "This is the end. We're going to have to break up. Everything is terrible."

After you share your issues with your partner, they might agree with you and say that they have also been experiencing these struggles. The two of you can then come up with methods to work through your biggest conflicts, and in the end, your relationship becomes even stronger. You don't break up; you stay together, and life is even better than ever before.

Professional Help

If you feel uncomfortable sharing your emotions with people in your life, start with professional help.

It can be overwhelming to try and find a therapist, but begin with your general practitioner. Go in for a checkup and talk about your symptoms of anger. Are you experiencing panic attacks? Do you have trouble sleeping at night? Is it hard for you to eat?

Discuss the symptoms with your doctor, and they can help create a plan for you. They might prescribe you an antidepressant or something that gives more of an immediate release. They might run tests and find that there's something simple that's the issue, like an irregular thyroid that can be treated with medication, diet, or exercise.

Anything physical could also have an impact on your emotional health, so start with this professional. After that, they can refer you to a therapist, a psychiatrist, or another mental health counselor who is able to come up with a plan for your anger.

While it can still feel scary to share your emotions even with the most professional medical experts, it's good to remember that this is their job. They've heard it all before. They've heard terrible thoughts from people. They've heard secrets that nobody else has ever heard. They've met wild characters, and they've experienced some of the darkest forms of mental health there are. Do not be afraid to open up to these professionals because that is exactly what they're there for. If you had one or two bad experiences with a doctor or therapist in the past, don't let this discourage you! They are still humans, and that can mean personalities clash. The right person is out there, and once you find them, you will feel immediate relief.

Problem-Solving Skills

Cognitive restructuring involves things like problem-solving skills, logic, and reasoning. When you face a problem, trace it back to the beginning. Look at all the possible solutions. Research these solutions and keep thinking up further ways that you can resolve your problems. Never settle for one solution.

For example, if you plan a date night with your partner only to discover that the movie theater is closed, the night isn't ruined. Can you have this fun date night at home? Can you enjoy a romantic walk in the park? Is there somewhere else that the two of you enjoy going to?

There are many solutions to your problems, even when it feels like there is only one.

Communication Skills

More important than learning how to express your emotions is learning how to be a good listener. If you're able to sit back and fully comprehend the things that the other person has to share with you, it's easier to maintain a healthy channel of communication between the two of you. This involves communication between you and your partner, you and your family members, or you and your co-workers.

Listening involves actually hearing what they're trying to say rather than hanging on to their words. Sometimes when people are listening to others, they focus on coming up with the right thing to say rather than actually hearing the message that the other person is sharing. Spend some time being mindful when the other person is talking, and always give them their chance to speak. Speaking over somebody and interrupting them is a form of control and can actually be very manipulative.

Trying to silence somebody else and not giving them a chance to share what they want is an attempt at having power in the situation. While it might seem like you are the one in control, in reality, the other person is simply too afraid to share what they're actually thinking. Open communication is based on honesty. Show the other person empathy and sympathy, and do your best to hear the things that they are saying.

When it comes to your form of communication, it's important to focus on “I feel” statements. If somebody wronged you in a way, don't call them out for specifically what they did wrong. Instead, focus on the emotions that you experienced. For example, perhaps your partner said that they were going to be home at 8 pm, but instead, they didn't come home until after midnight. Instead of saying, “You're always late. You're a bad partner. You don't care about me,” focus on your feelings.

Share things like, “I felt worried when I didn’t hear from you. I felt slightly disrespected that you didn’t think to call me.” If you focus on yourself, it makes the other person less likely to be defensive. If you call your partner a bad partner, they might get defensive and start listing reasons why you’re wrong, completely missing the point of the conflict. When you share your feelings, they can then respond by saying things like, “I’m sorry, my phone died, I’ll make sure it’s charged better next time.”

By implementing these long-term strategies into your life, it will be easier for you to have control over anger.

Avoidance

Although it's never good to avoid your problems, that doesn't mean that you always have to deal with everything the moment that it comes on. Sometimes you can simply close the door so that you don't see things that anger you or walk away from a situation that you know is going to set you off.

Avoidance shouldn't turn into suppression. However, it is a useful tactic for anger management. For example, if watching the news every single night makes you upset, then maybe avoid watching the news at night. Ask a partner to catch you up on major highlights, or wait until you are in a good mood to check in with the news.

In another example, let's say that your child is struggling to keep their room clean. Day after day, you walk by to see the chaotic mess, and it stresses you out. Shut the door so that you don't see the mess. Of course, you'll still want to talk to your child about keeping a clean area. You will want to set some rules with them or maybe even use a form of punishment like taking away computer time if they are not cleaning their room.

However, walking by it every day could trigger you to lash out at your child. You might also manifest that anger in other ways. For example, if you walk by their bedroom every single morning on your way to work, it can set your day off to a bad start. Have your child keep their door closed and deal with the issue when both of you are in the right headspace rather than having it become something that causes daily problems.

As another example, if your neighbor leaves a bright porch light on all night long that shines into your room, get blackout curtains.

Sure, you can fight with your neighbor all day. You can send them mean letters, you can take it to the city, and you can think up ways of revenge. But that causes long-term anger. Blackout curtains can help make sure that you get a good night's sleep without having them torture you on a daily basis.

Consider deleting all of your current apps and social media accounts, or at least temporarily deactivating them to help reduce feelings of anger. If the thought of this terrifies you or sounds like something that you are unable to do, there's a good chance that you are struggling with social media addiction. Apps provide instant gratification, so it's hard not to constantly scroll the internet, especially when you are able to do so with a little device that is constantly sitting in your pocket. Unfortunately, that can activate our hormones all day long, therefore disrupting our body's entire biological system. At the very least, start by turning off notifications. There's no reason that you need to get notified of new tweets, Instagram likes, or Reddit messages. Deactivate these notifications so that you can set specific times to go online. If you do still have to participate in using these apps, consider setting time limits. There are third-party apps to do this, or you can also do this on your own, depending on what type of phone you have. Setting a time limit would make sure that you're only spending a small amount of time on each social media app every single day rather than endlessly scrolling for hours.

Another trick to limit phone use is to set your screen to black and white. This makes colorful apps like Instagram or TikTok less exciting for your brain, so you might be less inclined to use them as frequently.

Avoidance can also happen within our daily routine. For example, if you get breakfast every morning at a certain restaurant, but they're constantly getting your order wrong, and it's making you mad, it's probably time to find a new restaurant. If you are driving to work and the same route you take every day is incredibly stressful, you might consider taking a different route, even if it takes an extra 10 minutes or adds a mile to your drive. It could save you a lot of emotional strain, and at the end of the day, that's much more valuable than anything else.

You might also consider taking things a step further and avoiding certain groups of people. If you go to a certain bar and you don't like the crowd because it gets rowdy at a specific time, it might be time to find a different bar. You might not want to find a new bar; it might be a reliable place that you've been going to for years. However, time changes things, and at a certain point, you have to embrace a new era in your life.

If your partner's friend group annoys you and you just don't vibe with their personalities, it's fine if you don't hang out with them every single time that they get together. In fact, your partner might actually appreciate having some alone time with their friends. While you might want to control the situation, you have to look internally and see if there is a power struggle going on with your emotions. Though you might feel left out, asking your partner to stop hanging out with this group of people is unfair and could damage your relationship.

If you find yourself repeatedly avoiding something, it's important to look at the deeper issues so that you don't suppress emotions. However, at the end of the day, remember that not every battle is one that you have to fight. Lions are known as being the king of the jungle, but even they will walk away from other predators or certain species that come into their territory. They know the importance of controlling their energy and reserving it for when it's actually needed. You don't have to fight every fight, and you don't have to power through every battle. Preserve your energy and do what is best to make sure that you maintain a peaceful emotional state.

Timing and Alternatives

Sometimes, confronting these battles means knowing when the time is right. For example, if you find that at night you are especially angry, and this is when you get into the most arguments with your partner, perhaps it's best to simply go to bed and wait until the morning to have certain discussions. Throughout the day. your hormones fluctuate, which means that can affect your emotional state. At night, you might be more tired, meaning that it's easier for you to be emotional.

Think about your mood when you get home from work. If you arrive at six o'clock, it might be six hours since you've had anything to eat, and maybe you're starving and ready for dinner. This might be a time when you come home angry and annoyed, but perhaps you simply need to eat before getting into a discussion with anybody. If this is the case, you can keep a small snack on you that you can eat during your commute home to ensure that you don't get home and start a fight with the family.

Learn how to find ways to decompress when you're off work. Perhaps you need to stop at a local park and sit outside on a bench while you do some breathing exercises before you go home. It doesn't mean that your home life is someplace that you want to avoid; transitioning from who you are at work to who you are at home can be emotionally exhausting. You might be somebody who has to be very serious or professional at work, but your home life is your sanctuary where you can be creative. Perhaps you're a doctor or a lawyer, and you're dealing with incredibly stressful things all day long. Trying to shift your mindset can be difficult, so it's very easy to bring work home with you. Find a way to decompress and have a moment before you transition from one mindset to the next.

For example, this could simply be sitting in your car and listening to a 30-minute meditation audiobook. Maybe you can call a friend and chat with them on your way home from work. You can talk about this with your partner so that they know when you get home to give you some time and space (remember that they might need this as well and to ensure both parties are getting proper relaxation time).

There's always a way to find an alternative to the things that are making you upset. How can you make this situation work for you? Emotional management means knowing how to use everything that passes through our brains in a positive and beneficial way.

Sometimes this is as simple as learning how to enjoy the moment. If you are stuck in traffic, it's easy to want to lay on your horn and scream at the other drivers in front of you. Instead, maybe this is the time to take a moment and simply sit with your feelings. Find a good radio station to play a song.

Plug in your phone and listen to that podcast or audiobook that you keep putting off. Simply turn the radio off, roll down your windows, and let the fresh air come into the car. Practice your breathing exercises and work through your thoughts. Take these moments where you have to be patient as gifts from the universe and let it be a sign that this is your chance to stop and take a breath.

It's always frustrating to feel like your time is being wasted, but when you let yourself get angry in that moment, you're going to end up wasting even more time.

Sure, you might have to sit in traffic for an hour, leaving you with the feeling that you'll never get those sixty minutes back. However, if you're angry, stewing, and frustrated to the point that you take this aggression home, that will waste much more time than that simple hour you lost to traffic.

Your personal time is just as precious as your personal peace. It's vital that you protect these things by establishing an alternative mindset where you can use your anger for good rather than letting it take more from your life.

CHAPTER 6:

Scenarios

There are many common situations that might trigger anger. We all face these things on a daily, weekly, or monthly basis. While you certainly have the ability to control your reactions, you won't always have the ability to stop anger-inducing situations from happening in the first place.

Stress can arise in countless common situations and it is normal for anger to follow. Instead of letting anger consume you, the long-term and short-term coping strategies we discussed above can help you. In addition, the scenarios below will provide examples of how you can take these practices and apply them to your real life.

Visualization is going to be one of the most beneficial tools you have to overcome anger. Go through all of these descriptive scenarios and stay mindful through each. Picture that you are in them and focus on deep breathing. If you have to take a break, that's fine too; you don't want to trigger yourself too much to the point that you elicit real, uncontrollable anger. Take it at your own pace and do your best to really see yourself in these scenarios so that if the issues arise in real life, you will be more prepared.

Road Rage

Driving is a common, everyday occurrence for many people. Many men also drive for their job. In fact, over 80% of commercial truck drivers are male (*Professional Truck Driver Demographics and Statistics in the U.S.*, n.d.). Learning how to deal with your own road rage, and aggression from other drivers, is important not just for your sanity but for your safety. Over 200 people have been murdered in road rage incidents in the past decade, and over 65% of accidents are caused by aggressive driving (Road Rage Statistics, 2023).

Scenario #1

It's a nice summer day. You and your partner drove an hour away to a gorgeous local beach. As you're riding happily on the highway in the right lane, a car passes you on the left. They get in front of you, only to slow down. You pass them on the left this time and return to the right lane. They end up passing you again, and this repeats for a few cycles until they change lanes a little too close in front of you, cutting you off and causing you to quickly tap the brakes. What do you do from here?

Anger Response: Speed up again, give them the finger, and cut them off.

Better Response: Briefly honk your horn to make them alert if they are being careless. Slow down until they've gone far ahead of you, and carry on with the rest of your drive.

Scenario #2

You're already late for work, and you can't find your keys. Eventually, you find them in yesterday's pants in the hamper, and you rush out of the door. As you turn down the street towards your work, a car is parked idling in the middle of the street.

Anger Response: Get out of the car to wait for them to return and start a physical/verbal altercation once they do.

Better Response: Check the clock and wait a moment as you search for the driver. In big cities, sometimes it's the only option for deliveries. Most people return within 1-3 minutes, which doesn't make a huge difference, and maybe it's the delivery driver's first day on a new job. If there is no sign of anyone around after a few minutes, honk your horn to alert them.

Kids and Partners

There are many types of triggering situations that you might find yourself and your family in the middle of. It's important to learn how to control your anger to protect your family and ensure that you get the most out of your home life. Intimate partner violence is more likely to lead to depression and anxiety (Statistics, n.d.). Another devastating statistic shows that "A study of intimate partner homicides found that 20% of victims were not the intimate partners themselves, but family members, friends, neighbors, persons who intervened, law enforcement responders, or bystanders" (Statistics, n.d.).

Also, over 70% of murder-suicides are among intimate partners, with 94% of the victims being female (Statistics, n.d.).

In addition to these statistics, 1 in 15 children is exposed to partner violence in their lifetime (Statistics, n.d.). Over 100,000 children are abused by their fathers every year (Number of Child Abuse Victims in the United States in 2021, By Perpetrator Relationship, 2021).

Statistics like these shouldn't make us feel bad about being men. Instead, they should highlight the importance of why we need to take back control over our emotions. This isn't crucial just for us, but for our families as well. We have the power to influence friends, family members, and our children to be better sons, fathers, brothers, and members of society.

Scenario #3

You, your wife, and your two children spent the day at your nephew's birthday party. The day was filled with games, laughter, and plenty of candy. Now that you're home, the kids refuse to go to bed. Your toddler starts to have a meltdown and begins running around the house, yelling, and crying

Anger Response: You scream at the children and carry them into their room, slamming the door and repeating this cycle until everyone is exhausted and crying.

Better Response: You offer to read your children a bedtime story as long as they calm down and get under the covers. You grab a glass of water for yourself, practice deep breathing, and avoid reacting to them until they eventually give in and crawl into bed. You wait for their emotions to cool off and read them a brief story. It only takes a few pages for the sugar rush to wear off, and they're fast asleep.

Scenario #4

It's your girlfriend's birthday weekend, and you find out her friend is throwing her a party at a restaurant you can't stand.

Anger Response: Skip the party altogether, or if you go, you are resentful and give the silent treatment most of the night. Eventually, you both get into a fight when you get home.

Better Response: Sneak out to grab a quick meal before you both head to the restaurant. Get her a surprise too, while you're out, and remember not to take it as a personal attack. Her friend is doing something nice for her, and you can still enjoy the party even if you don't like the food.

Anger Response: Yell at them, throw the popcorn, and tell them you're never coming back again.

Better Response: Let them know you don't want one or two of the items if you don't want to spend the money. The cashier at the theater can't control the prices. If you're still upset, you can consider sending a message on the corporate website to let them know of your grievances.

Scenario #8

It's been a long day, so you and your partner decide to go to your favorite fast-food restaurant as a treat. You check your order after the drive-thru to see that they forgot one of your sandwiches.

Anger Response: Blare your horn in the drive-thru until they come out and give you your sandwich.

Better Response: Park your car, walk into the restaurant, and politely let them know you're missing an item. Most of the time, they will replace the item or at least give you a refund for the missing item.

Social Media

Social media gives us access to unlimited information. Some of this can make us feel better. Other times, it can be incredibly triggering to our anger. In fact, some social media algorithms are specifically designed to provide you with anger-inducing content because it helps drive engagement (NPR, 2022). If you see a controversial post, you might be more likely to read the comments or share it with friends. Because of this, it can create an online world where you are constantly fed triggering information. Let's look at some of these scenarios to help give you a full picture of the reality of the online world.

Scenario #9

Your alarm goes off, and you keep hitting the snooze button. When you finally roll out of bed, you open your phone and check the news right away.

Anger Response: You get upset about what you see and go on a deep dive into the subject, procrastinating getting ready for work.

Better Response: You take some time to wake up since you were already struggling to do so that morning. You skip checking your messages and instead take a hot shower to get a level head.

Scenario #10

You see a headline that says [Insert a celebrity you dislike] said [something ridiculous].

Anger Response: Comment something negative on the post and tell everyone you talk to that day about this headline.

Better Response: Click on the article to see that it was a sensationalized headline, or decide to keep scrolling and ignore the post altogether.

Additional Scenarios

Additional Scenarios:

Use the same format from the previous situations to fill in the blanks for these scenarios on your own (What are the anger/better responses?):

1.Someone comments something negative on your Instagram post.

2.You see a text pop up on your partner's phone, and it's from their ex.

3.Your boss gave a promotion to your coworker when you thought you would get it.

4. Your coworker won't stop smacking their gum and gossiping loudly around the office.

5. Your child comes home with a bad report card.

6. The dog used the bathroom in the house, and one of your children walked through it, dragging it across the carpet.

7. You break a casserole dish as you put it in the dishwasher.

8. The dryer stops working five minutes after you loaded it with sopping wet clothes.

9. Your favorite sports team loses within the last two minutes of a game where they had been doing well the entire time.

10. You arrive at a hotel to check in on vacation, only to find that they "lost" your reservation.

Practice visualizing these and other situations so that you can be prepared to respond in the appropriate way.

CHAPTER 7:

Make a Plan

What will help me overcome anger once and for all?

A plan is important for building good habits and making progress around managing your anger. Sticking to a plan will lead to long-term success.

Now that you've made it through the rest of the chapters, what information has stuck with you the most? It's time to use this and form a plan around how you will attack your anger. This way, once you become aware of your emotional state, it will be easier to know exactly what to do next rather than acting on impulse. The lessons learned in previous chapters are used to develop a personal strategy that you can stick to in order to control your anger. You will be happier in the long term by reiterating what to do, knowing what the plan is, and sticking to it.

Coping Strategies

Coping strategies are the main things that you do when you first become aware of that initial anger emotion. Right now, take some time to identify the coping strategies that you have and whether or not they are helping reduce your anger or if they are only creating bigger problems. For example, if you cope by using drugs, alcohol, sex, or even violence, this can only make the problem worse while also adding other stressors to your life. Once you're able to identify the current coping strategies you have, it'll be easier to know how to follow the good coping strategies.

For example, if you're somebody who binge eats late at night because of stress about work the next day, you can recognize this while you are in the right mindset. Then, as the night approaches, you can get ahead of your emotions and use a healthier coping mechanism. In this situation, perhaps you decide to try going for a peaceful night walk or enjoying some music and warm tea on the balcony. While it might not be as instantly rewarding as excessive food, it'll make you feel so much better the next day. The relief of the next day is rewarding enough for you to want to keep following the healthier coping strategy.

Unhealthy coping mechanisms you currently have might include:

- excessive sleep
- drug/alcohol use
- spending impulsively on shopping sprees/large purchases
- disordered eating, such as binging and purging
- gambling
- phone use/social media
- isolation
- denial/avoidance

Healthier alternatives are things like:

- socializing
- exercising
- writing
- drawing/painting
- playing a game or puzzle (ie. crossword and jigsaw puzzles or board games)
- self-care like a hot bath or using a massage gun

- gardening
- reading

To help lead you to these healthy coping mechanisms when in the face of anger, start by counting to ten.

Count to Ten

Prepared short-term coping strategies can be practiced even when you are in the right mindset. As someone who's struggled with anger management, you know that the advice of "counting to 10" can sound repetitive. Whether it was a parent or friend who told you this, it can be annoying to hear in the heat of the moment.

We've all been in a situation where we were too angry to display this momentary mindfulness. The best thing to do is to practice this at times when you are not angry so that it has more meaning to you in the moments when you are.

When you practice counting to ten, you're giving yourself a pause so that the emotions can regulate themselves. Remember that anger is a chemical reaction, so if you take a second to calm down, it can slow the hormone release. This strategy ensures that your heartbeat is regulated and your breathing will become consistent rather than sped up.

A helpful way to remember this strategy is to go through the 10 parts of anger in your body. These are your:

- mind
- eyes
- breath
- shoulders
- neck
- chest
- heart

- arms
- fists
- legs

Start with your mind. Anger sparks in the mind and your thoughts. Try and pause your mind for a moment as reality sets in.

Focus on your eyes. As you're on this second part, close your eyes for a moment, blink, and get a better sense of your surroundings. Anger can cause tunnel vision, so if you take a second to refocus, it can give you a clearer vision of the real issues that you're confronting.

Notice your breath. Breathe in through your nose and out through your mouth. Alternate which nostril you use by taking turns closing each side with your pinky by pressing down. Breathe in and out.

Fourth, look at your shoulders. Are they tense? Are they rising? Are they touching your ears? Move them in backward circles to help you relax them. Pretend you have something on your back you're trying to shake off.

Next, think about your neck. Twist your head around in a few circular motions to help release some of the tension in your neck. If you are doing this even when you are peaceful, it helps create a more consistent pattern so that you're able to follow through these steps when you're feeling angry.

Sixth, think about your chest. Is your chest rising? Is your chest tense? Are you leaning forward and hunching over? Is your chest feeling tight and sore? If you relax your chest, it can also help you move on to the next part, which involves your heart.

Keep focusing on your breathing and feel your heart. Is it racing? Is it beating extra hard? Try to slow down and visualize your heart rate decreasing.

Eighth, look at your arms. Are they tense? Are they crossed? Are you holding them up? Are you waving them around? Relax your arms and let them hang loosely.

That takes us down to the ninth part of anger, your fists. Are you clenching your fists? Are you holding your arms and your fists really tight? Let them relax.

Lastly, think about your legs. If you've gone through all nine of these parts of your body and you're still feeling uncontrollable anger, use your legs to walk away. That is the best thing that you will be able to do in the heat of the moment.

Visualize this descending pattern once again. Think of a peaceful wave passing through your mind, eyes, breath, shoulders, neck, chest, heart, arms, fists, and legs. Use your legs to walk away if you're still standing in front of the thing that's making you angry. This coping strategy can be one of the most beneficial ways for you to manage your anger in the short term.

Sometimes this isn't enough, and even getting here can be difficult. Let's talk about a few more immediate actions that you can take when anger is out of control.

Immediate Actions

Coping strategies do not always work immediately, so a plan for immediate action should be in place. For example, as we discussed in the previous section, walk away from a situation in which you are going to yell at your wife before you do the actual yelling.

Beyond this, simply saying the emotion to yourself can be enough for you to bring awareness. When you're upset, and you feel your heart pounding, simply think of the word "anger." Once you're able to say the word, you can use the actual acronym ANGER to help you calm down. Trace the letters in your mind and think of the associated word for each part:

- awareness
- nose breathing
- go
- effort
- regret

A is used to help yourself spark awareness in the moment. Who are you fighting with, and what is the real conflict here? What are either of you going to gain by following through with your anger?

N stands for nose breathing. Breathe in and breathe out. Breathe in and breathe out. Keep using your nose, and it will help your mind focus on your surroundings rather than acting impulsively on your emotions.

G stands for go. Get out of the situation, and leave as fast as you can. Use your legs to get up and go to your safe space. Sometimes this is not enough if you're stuck in the same place as the other person, you might want to return to the situation and fight with them further. That takes us to the next letter.

E stands for effort. Make the effort to stay where you are. Don't return to the fight, even if it's with your spouse that you can't avoid in the other room. Put in the work, be strong, and be resilient. Once you calm down and get your thoughts straight, you can return, but for now, put some effort into calming down.

R stands for regret. Finally, when all of these other letters aren't working for you, think about regret. Think about the past regrets that you have related to anger, and envision the things that you wish you would have done differently. Now is your chance to do the right thing! This will give you instant insight into what the best thing to do in this situation is so that you can prevent further damage.

Acronyms like this, and the 10 parts of anger, can be hard to keep up with when you're in that moment and feeling rage. It's not always easy to stop and go through a list in your mind. However, simply saying the word or thinking about counting to ten can at least distract your mind from the trigger to get the process of emotional awareness started.

Anger Words

In addition to this, another immediate action that you can take is to have a safe word or an “anger” word for the people who are going to be around you. If you're going on a vacation with your family, it might be an overwhelming and stressful time. Have a safe word with your partner so that if you're feeling triggered, you can share this with them, and it'll be easier for everybody to understand that it's time to stop arguing before it gets worse. In addition, if you need to leave the room, they will understand exactly why.

Even if you have to abruptly stop a conversation and use the anger word to walk away, that is better than letting it escalate into a fight. Of course, if you're saying the word multiple times a day, every single day, it may turn into an avoidant habit. As you are in the beginning stages of anger management, it can be helpful to de-escalate heated situations.

Anger Objects

It can also be beneficial if you keep an anger object on you. This can be something small. Maybe it's the bottle cap of your favorite beer. Perhaps it's a stone that you find on a peaceful walk. Find something small that you can keep in your pocket at all times. When you are feeling happy, excited, and/or positive about your anger management, hold this object.

Pass it between your hands, rub it with your fingers, squeeze it with your hands, and feel it in your pocket. Then when you are angry, you can touch this object, and you will be able to remember the feelings that you have when you are happy and positive. This way, it will create mindfulness around the situation and make it easier for you to reduce feelings of anger.

Anger Phrases

Find a phrase that has power to you. Repeat it to yourself even when you're happy. Maybe it's a song lyric that you like or a quote by somebody that you look up to. Keep it short and simple. Consider positive affirmations like:

- I am a good person.
- I am braver than my anger.
- I can do this.
- I am strong.
- I am brave.

If you can repeat these things to yourself when you're in a good mood, they will have more power over your emotional state when you're in a bad mood. You could even write this phrase down on your anger object to help keep you even more mindful.

It's important to practice using quick phrases as well. These might be things like:

- I can't talk right now.
- I need a minute.
- I'm sorry, I have to go away.
- I need to be alone right now.
- I'm feeling overstimulated.
- I'm feeling overwhelmed.

Pick "I" statements that you can share with the other person and simply walk away. They might feel like it's rude if you have to leave abruptly. However, it's better to apologize for the abruptness later rather than let it escalate into an argument that takes days or weeks to overcome.

Keep Counting

When you are feeling trapped in a room, and it feels like there's not much you can do, find something that you can physically count. Think about this right now. How many lights are in the room? How many chairs? How many things are made out of wood? How many things are your favorite color?

Sometimes you can't get up and leave the situation, so you can find an object or pattern in the room to keep you mindful. How many tiles are on the wall? How many flowers are in the patterned carpet? Count as high as you can. By the time you reach ten, 50, or 100, you will notice that many of the angering thoughts in your mind have subsided.

By identifying these things around you, your mind will be pulled from the angry pool of rage it's drowning in and instead return to the surface, the present moment.

Cold Therapy

Another immediate response is a cold shower. If you're home, hop into the shower right away and let the cold shock you momentarily. This will pull all of your focus from your angry mindset and instead place it right in the peaceful shower. Spend 5-10 minutes in the cold shower. Start with small increments and increase over time.

If you don't have the chance to get wet, start with your face. Go to the breakroom at the office and stick your head in the freezer. Fill a bowl of ice water at home and dunk your face for ten seconds, or for however long you can hold your breath if you can't make it to ten.

You can try using cold therapy as a long-term method as well. Fill your bathtub with cold water and ice cubes (or ice packs to be more environmentally friendly). This can help you practice having power over your body and thoughts. Anger management is important to keep up with both in the short and long term.

Continued Practice

The coping strategies and quick plan implementations are incredibly beneficial for your anger management. What is going to be the most helpful thing for you, however, is to continually practice reducing feelings of anger. Going forward, this should be one of your main prioritizations.

This can start by simply visualizing an angry situation at home to help you practice your reaction. Exposure therapy can be very beneficial because if you let yourself live from moment to moment, it can make you more impulsive. Visualizing the situation in the future helps create reality in your brain, and it makes you less emotionally reactive when that situation arises.

While it can be triggering at times, it's also important to talk about past experiences. Start by writing them down on your phone or by using a journal. Writing can be a very expressive way to help you get all of your emotions out. Just be cautious that you're in the right headspace when you do this so as not to trigger your anger even further.

Setbacks and Further Mistakes

Remember that if you do run into setbacks, don't get discouraged. You know now exactly how to get out of the trap that you might have fallen into. Mistakes are opportunities for us to learn. Of course, we should always try to avoid making them in the first place, but know that there will be setbacks in this process.

If you make a mistake, don't think of it as taking two steps back because setbacks are an expected part of the process. There will be times when you stay stuck in one place, but no matter what, when you take your health into your own hands, you're already a step ahead of where you used to be.

Each experience is another situation that you can add to your big book of life lessons. One mistake doesn't undo all of the good work that you've done, and it shouldn't validate the belief that you are a broken or unfixable person; it's simply a reminder that you are human and that you still are feeling your emotions. Now you know how to avoid that again in future situations.

If you keep making the same mistakes over and over again, it's important to look deeper at what the core issue is. If something isn't working, then it needs to change. You can't expect change to happen on your own, so it's vital to take the initiative and have self-discipline when you are repeatedly experiencing the same setbacks.

Relaxation Techniques

Incorporate more relaxation techniques long term. Don't wait until you're stressed out to relax. Relaxation should happen in some form every single day. Whether it's simply watching a movie at night, or taking a hot bath, make sure that your body is experiencing these moments of peace to help regulate your hormones. Try meditation. You can find many free meditation scripts or videos online, or you can purchase meditation audiobooks. Meditation is also something that you can do completely on your own, but guided meditation can help you learn how to do it first.

Sit in a peaceful place with no music, no lights, and no sound at all. Make sure there are no distractions and find a comfortable spot to lie. Close your eyes. Let yourself think thoughts but don't expand on them. Think of it like you are riding the bus and simply looking out of the window at all of the stores, restaurants, and other businesses on the street. As you ride the bus, you don't stop and get off. You don't walk into any of these stores. You're simply sitting there, riding past them all, and letting them flow by. Focus on your breathing and start with five-minute intervals. Over time, extend it to ten minutes. Before you know it, you'll be able to meditate for 30 minutes to an hour.

It's also important to find a hobby for you to have an emotional release. Artistic hobbies are great places to start, whether it's writing, drawing, or painting. Think about athletic hobbies as well. You can even find a partner to help keep you accountable. Try out a new sport like tennis.

Sign up at your local gym or community center to use the pool and go swimming. Get into woodworking or try building your own instrument. There are so many hobbies for you to explore, and if you find something that you can be passionate about, it helps motivate you. It provides more evidence that you are a good person deserving of healing.

Self-Care

Don't neglect self-care. Often this can be associated with femininity, but everybody deserves to feel good about themselves and to care for themselves. This includes things like taking a hot bubble bath.

Splurge on yourself. Treat yourself to a massage or a trip to the spa. Save up to buy self-care equipment like a hot tub or sauna. These things are expensive, but putting effort toward a long-term goal like this can boost your confidence and give you something to look forward to. Get a straight razor shave at a barber shop and enjoy the hot towel after.

These types of things not only relax your body, but also show your mind that you care about yourself. The best way to make sure that you're keeping up with these coping strategies and continually practicing anger management is to create your physical plan and implement it.

Plan Implementation

Take time to write your plan down. Use a notebook or a computer program to document the things you want to do. Create a chart, spreadsheet, or illustration of what you plan to do. This can be adapted to your own preference and style. Use something that works for you and that you can go back to as needed. Write down things like

- big triggers for anger.
- small frustrations to overcome.
- coping mechanisms that you currently have.
- coping mechanisms you hope to adapt.
- people you can trust.
- short-term solutions.
- long-term solutions.

Share your plan with those you feel safe doing so with. They can keep you accountable, and they can ask about how your plan is going and if you believe things are improving. This will give you a chance to have a real outside source that helps keep you in line with your plan.

Create goals so that you have something to measure. These might include things like

- have zero outbursts over 90 days.
- reconnect with a friend that anger drove away.
- meditate daily for a week.
- sign up for a yoga class.

Create goals that are specific to you, and that will help you reduce feelings of anger. This is important so that you have something physical to look back on to see if you are following through with your wants. This will keep you more accountable and can help improve self-discipline if you find that you are struggling to keep up. Remind yourself when things go well, and let yourself feel good about that. Reward yourself once you reach milestones to serve as an additional reminder of why all of this effort is worth it in the end.

There will be times when you are triggered by anger once again, but don't get disappointed if this happens. It's easy to beat yourself up and think things like, "Why did I let that bother me?" or, "I should have known better." It's disappointing to see so much progress and then fall back into an old habit. Remind yourself that this is normal, and as long as it's not a constant occurrence, you are still healing and becoming better.

Create awareness of how others might display their anger. Using others as an example can help you create awareness around your own habits. It will keep you mindful of how others might perceive you, making it easier to improve your social awareness and social skills.

Some of what you practiced visualizing may help already! You are already further along on this journey than some people will ever be, and that is certainly something to be proud of.

Seeking Additional Help

You are capable of this journey. You are strong, you are powerful, and you are intelligent. You took the initiative to start the journey of helping yourself. Anger is an emotion, and emotions are based on feelings. Feelings are based on thoughts, and everything is connected to one another. This means that you have the power within your own mind to help manage some of your most complicated feelings. While you might be able to have this realization, how do you know if you need to seek additional help?

The simple answer is that everybody will benefit from help. Sometimes the best way you can help yourself is to reach out to others. If you're somebody who has had anger management issues at any time in your life, seeking support through therapy is going to be beneficial to you.

It can feel strange at first, and it might be something that isn't normalized in your life, but you will be amazed at just how helpful it can be. Even if you only need a few months of therapy and then you start to feel better already, at least you tried.

Unfortunately, health care can be hard to access for some people, so it might not be something that you can necessarily prioritize in your life. Remember that your mental health is just as important as your physical health. If you had a broken bone, you wouldn't put off going to the doctor. If you were having a heart attack, you wouldn't try and handle it on your own. Why is mental health any different?

You never know how serious something might get or where your thoughts might lead you, so it's always better to get help before it's too late. If you're still skeptical and unsure of whether or not you need help, there are a few signs that can certainly point to the severity of your situation.

If you find yourself blacking out and having moments where you don't remember what happened, it's important to seek help immediately. It could be a sign that there is a larger issue, such as Intermittent Explosive Disorder (*Intermittent Explosive Disorder*, n.d.). Blacking out is never a good thing, and if you're unsure of what actions you might have taken in the past, then that means that there is no way of controlling what you might do in the future. It's important to talk to somebody immediately if you are blacking out during fits of rage.

In addition, it's essential that you seek help if you have been physically violent towards somebody else. This is especially true if it is a domestic violence situation. If you have ever physically hurt your partner or a family member, you should seek help immediately. You might be afraid because you don't want to get in legal trouble. However, you are going to get in so much more legal trouble in the future if the situation escalates into something further than what it already has.

Third, seek professional help if you are struggling with an addiction. Even if it doesn't seem like it's related to your anger, there are a lot more connections than you may realize. It's so incredibly important to seek help when trying to overcome addiction. You will have days where you feel like you can do it all on your own, but at other moments it will be incredibly hard.

Seek help if your anger issues become noticeable to other people. If somebody mentions it to you, it's time to talk to a professional. If your boss, a friend, or your partner tells you that they believe you have anger issues, this in itself can be very triggering to your anger. We want to have control over our lives, and somebody else telling us how we feel or how we act can make us feel like we are losing some of that autonomy. However, even though you might disagree with them or you might not want them to be right, when somebody else is able to acknowledge that there are anger issues involved, then it is usually a good thing to believe them.

Seek help early on so that you can make sure any further damage from your anger is prevented. Therapy can come in all shapes and sizes. You can have individual weekly sessions. You can have virtual sessions. You can even try types of group therapy. This helps you connect to and relate to others and feel less alone in your struggles.

There are also many online resources that you can find in your area, depending on where you live, and if you're ever unsure of what to do, always reach out through help and crisis hotlines. Emotions are felt in our head first, and often that can make us minimize them. However, it's always best to get on top of your health before it turns into something worse.

CONCLUSION

Anger is something that, at this point in your life, might have only been associated with negativity. You might have lost friendships, relationships, and job opportunities because of angry outbursts or rage-induced moments.

Getting to a point where you admit that you have anger problems can feel very scary. To do this, you have to admit that you don't have control over everything. Often, anger is the very thing that we use to try and make us feel as though we have control.

Where you are right now in life is proof that you do have power. You have power over your decisions. You are able to make a choice. You know the right thing to do. Deep down, the just thing to do, the truth, and your moral beliefs will always be somewhere in your mind. Anger can make it hard to find them, but buried inside of you always exists the right thing to do.

Now it is up to you to make sure that everything else that clouds your judgment stays away. Other people are going to egg you on and frustrate you. You are going to hear upsetting and enraging news on a daily basis. You are going to be triggered at work and while you're driving to and from your job.

You now know, deep down, that the best thing to do is to calm down and maintain a level head. Everything else that triggers you is simply a test. A challenge between who you are now and the version of yourself that you want to be. You are braver than this, and you are more intelligent than anything that gets in your way of living a peaceful and serene life.

Anger is normal and common. It is natural, and it's a biological feeling that every single human has felt before. Anybody who says that they have never been angry is likely lying to themselves. Some of these people might be the angriest people that you'll ever meet.

As a man, you experience anger in a different way because of what society has done to men. The pressures placed on us, the perceptions created around us, and our ability to share our emotions have done damaging things to our mental and physical health.

The impact of anger on the way that your body operates can have detrimental effects. Now it is time for you to take back power over your health and live the calm life you deserve.

Remember to always work on your emotional intelligence. Name your emotions and understand where they came from. Identify the thought patterns and the endless cycles that keep you stuck in the same old mindset. Allow your brain to grow and flourish in the way that you deserve, to get the life that you've always dreamed of.

Remember to create awareness around the environmental factors that trigger you. Sometimes simply removing yourself from the situation or finding an alternative is enough for you to mitigate your anger.

Practice short-term strategies even when you are not angry. Create normalcy around implementing different methods and practical ways for you to take back control over the way that you feel. Visualize different scenarios that you will be in so that you are able to not only create a strong plan but implement it with positive effects.

Life doesn't have to be an angry and rageful place. There will always be reasons to validate feelings of anger, but at the end of the day, the person who suffers the most is you. Your mind can be your biggest enemy, but it can also be your greatest tool.

You deserve to be free from anxiety, fear, anger, rage, disappointment, and frustration. Negative emotions are inevitable, but the downfall that can follow is something that you have the power to prevent. Anger can be managed, and the process has already started. Now it is up to you to make the right choice every day to become the person that you wish to be.

Thank you for reading my book! I hope this book helped you whether it was life changing or added a little bit of good advice to your life.

Please leave a review if you would like to help others with this book. It only takes a minute!

amzn.to/3LDuswW

OR

SCAN

REFERENCES

10 Types of Anger. (2019). Modern Therapy. https://moderntherapy.online/blog-2/2019/3/31/types-of-anger

Albrecht, K. (2012). *The (Only) 5 Fears We All Share*. Psychology Today. https://www.psychologytoday.com/us/blog/brainsnacks/201203/the-only-5-fears-we-all-share

American Heart Association. (n.d.). *How High Blood Pressure Can Lead to Vision Loss*. Heart. https://www.heart.org/en/health-topics/high-blood-pressure/health-threats-from-high-blood-pressure/how-high-blood-pressure-can-lead-to-vision-loss#:~:text=HBP%20can%20harm%20your%20eyesight%20in%20many%20ways&text=Blood%20vessel%20damage%20(retinopathy)%3A,risk%20for%20developing%20this%20condition.

Anger - How it Affects People. (n.d.). Better Health Channel. https://www.betterhealth.vic.gov.au/health/healthyliving/anger-how-it-affects-people

Anger Statistics. (n.d.). Mind Your Anger. https://www.mindyouranger.com/anger/anger-statistics/

Anger Statistics. (n.d.). Mind Your Anger. https://www.mindyouranger.com/anger/anger-statistics/

Are Women Literally Dying Of Embarrassment?. (2018). Her Heart. https://herheart.org/dying-of-embarrassment/

Aspects of Anger. (n.d.). APS. https://psychology.org.au/for-the-public/psychology-topics/managing-your-anger/why-do-we-get-angry#:~:text=The%20sympathetic%20nervous%20system%20is,the%20sensation%20of%20feeling%20hot.

Cuncic, A. (2022). *The Connection Between Depression and Anger.* Verywell Mind. https://www.verywellmind.com/connection-between-depression-and-anger-5085725

Delvin, H.. (2019). *Science of Anger: How Gender, Age and Personality Shape This Emotion.* The Guardian. https://www.theguardian.com/lifeandstyle/2019/may/12/science-of-anger-gender-age-personality

Eating Disorders in Males. (n.d.). Eating Disorder Hope. https://www.eatingdisorderhope.com/risk-groups/men#:~:text=25%25%20of%20those%20diagnosed%20with,alter%20their%20weight%20%5B1%5D.

Eliot, L. (n.d.). *Brain Development and Physical Aggression*. The University of Chicago Press. https://www.journals.uchicago.edu/doi/full/10.1086/711705#:~:text=Learning%2C%20or%20neuroplasticity%2C%20is%20both,more%20physically%20aggressive%20than%20women.

FBI. (20112). *Crime in the United States.* FBI:UCR. https://ucr.fbi.gov/crime-in-the-u.s/2012/crime-in-the-u.s.-2012/tables/42tabledatadecoverviewpdf/table_42_arrests_by_sex_2012.xls

Fisher, L. (n.d.). *Can You Die of Embarrassment?* Science Focus. https://www.sciencefocus.com/the-human-body/can-you-die-of-embarrassment/

Gender and Crime. (n.d.). Study Smarter. https://www.studysmarter.us/explanations/social-studies/crime-

and-deviance/gender-and-crime/#:~:text=Biological%20explanations%20focus%20on%20the,aggressive%20and%2For%20criminal%20behaviour.

Gerster, J. (2020). *More Men Are Killed Than Women, So Why Focus On Violence Against Women?.* Global News. https://globalnews.ca/news/6536184/gender-based-violence-men-women/

Golen, T. (2022). *Could Stress Be Making My Acid Reflux Worse?.* Harvard Health Publishing. https://www.health.harvard.edu/newsletter_article/could-stress-be-making-my-acid-reflux-worse#:~:text=Emotional%20stress%20can%20increase%20acid,)%20doesn't%20work%20properly.

Hartmans, A. (2021). *How The Simple Phrase 'the Customer Is Always Right' Gave Shoppers A License To Abuse Workers.* Business Insider. https://www.businessinsider.com/customer-is-always-right-etail-worker-violence-harassment-2021-9

Heshmat, S. (2018). *The 10 Key Ingredients of Anger.* Psychology Today. https://www.psychologytoday.com/us/blog/science-choice/201812/the-10-key-ingredients-anger

How Stress & Anxiety Affect Your Gut. (2022). Northeast Digestive. https://www.northeastdigestive.com/blog/how-stress-affects-your-stomach/#:~:text=One%20stress%20hormone%2C%20in%20particular,example%2C%20causing%20sudden%20stomach%20cramps

Intermittent Explosive Disorder. (n.d.). Cleveland Clinic. https://my.clevelandclinic.org/health/diseases/17786-intermittent-explosive-disorder

Johnson, S. (2016). *Anger, Shame, Explosive Rage And Violence: When Men Act Out Their Pain.* Stephen J. Johnson, Ph.D. https://drstephenjohnson.com/2016/07/11/anger-shame-explosive-rage-and-violence-when-men-act-out-their-stress/

Kelsh, C. (2015). *Are Criminal Courts More Lenient on Women?* The Journalist's Resource. https://journalistsresource.org/criminal-justice/courts-lenient-sentencing-bond-women/

Khatri, M. (2022). *Slideshow: The Truth About Sugar Addiction.* Nourish by WebMD. https://www.webmd.com/diet/ss/slideshow-sugar-addiction

Litvak, P., Lerner, J., Tiedens, L., and Shonk, K.. (2010). *Fuel in the Fire: How Anger Impacts Judgment and Decision-Making.* International Handbook of Anger. https://scholar.harvard.edu/files/jenniferlerner/files/fuel_in_the_fire_how_anger_impacts_judgment_and_decision_making_0.pdf

McMurray, F. (2022). *'Anger Led Me to Prison'.* The Crime Report. https://thecrimereport.org/2022/02/25/anger-led-me-to-prison/

Men and Emotions. (n.d.). MensLine Australia. https://mensline.org.au/mens-mental-health/men-and-emotions/

Merriam-Webster. (n.d.). *Anger.* Merriam-Webster. https://www.merriam-webster.com/dictionary/anger

Miller, M. (n.d.). *Getting Unstuck: The Power of Naming Emotions.* 6 Seconds. https://www.6seconds.org/2021/01/08/getting-unstuck-power-naming-emotions/

NPR. (2022). *Does Social Media Leave You Feeling Angry? That Might Be Intentional.* NPR. https://www.npr.org/2022/09/13/1122786134/does-social-media-leave-you-feeling-angry-that-might-be-intentional

Number Of Child Abuse Victims In The United States In 2021, By Perpetrator Relationship. (2021). Statista. https://www.statista.com/statistics/254893/child-abuse-in-the-us-by-perpetrator-relationship/

Ohwovoriole, T. (2021). *What is Anger?*. Verywell Mind. https://www.verywellmind.com/what-is-anger-5120208

Priato, D. (2020). *7 Harmful Effects of Overeating.* Healthline. https://www.healthline.com/nutrition/overeating-effects

Professional Truck Driver Demographics and Statistics in the U.S. (n.d.). Zippia. https://www.zippia.com/professional-truck-driver-jobs/demographics/

Road Rage Statistics. (2023). The Zebra. https://www.thezebra.com/resources/research/road-rage-statistics/

Serotonin Levels Affect The Brain's Response To Anger. (2011). University of Cambridge. https://www.cam.ac.uk/research/news/serotonin-levels-affect-the-brain%E2%80%99s-response-to-anger

Statistics. (n.d.). NCADV. https://ncadv.org/STATISTICS

Strong, D. (2015). *7 Ways Anger is Ruining Your Health.* https://www.everydayhealth.com/news/ways-anger-ruining-your-health/

Suicide Statistics. (2022). American Foundation for Suicide Prevention. https://afsp.org/suicide-statistics/

Taylor, K. (2019). *More Retail Workers Than Law-Enforcement Officers Were Killed in Homicides on the Job for 6 Years in a Row.* Business Insider. https://www.businessinsider.com/more-retail-workers-police-officers-killed-homicides-2019-8

Tjan, A. (2015). *5 Ways to Become More Self-Aware.* Harvard Business Review. https://hbr.org/2015/02/5-ways-to-become-more-self-aware

Upham, B. (2023). *Childhood Trauma May Lead to Anger in Adulthood.* Everyday Health. https://www.everydayhealth.com/emotional-health/childhood-trauma-may-lead-to-anger-in-adulthood/

WebMD. (2021). *Slideshow: Erectile Dysfunction Causes.* WebMD. https://www.webmd.com/men/ss/slideshow-causes-of-ed

White, E. (2013). *Inside The Minds Of Murderers: Impulsive Murderers Much More Mentally Impaired Than Those Who Kill Strategically.* Science Daily. https://www.sciencedaily.com/releases/2013/06/130627131835.htm

Made in the USA
Middletown, DE
14 July 2024

57293552R00070